HO|

MW01591517

THE

CHILDREN!

Reflections of a Lifetime in the People Business

by

Peter Fiore
(And His People)

{ 1 }

TABLE OF CONTENTS

INTRODUCTION

This is a book about a career in education.

This is a book about catharsis.

This is a book about magic.

This is a book about redemption.

This is a book about relationships.

This is a book about reflection.

This is a book about simplicity.

This is a book about consistency.

This is a book about paying it forward.

Most importantly, this is a book about love.

Over three years have elapsed from my retirement as a classroom teacher, a career which spanned twenty years spread over four decades. I saw a lot, I learned a lot, I screwed up a lot, and I succeeded a lot.

Many of my first students from the 1970's are now parents and grandparents. Others from the 21st century have also started families of their own. Perhaps some of them will recount experiences we shared in school with their offspring, and perhaps not. No matter. This work is dedicated to all of them.

I suppose practically anyone would get something out of this piece. After all, everyone went to school, and most of us likely had problems at one time or another, either with a subject, a teacher, a bully, or whatever.

I do not profess to have the answer to every educational question or concern, as the problems are myriad. Hell, I don't even know half the questions, let alone the proper responses. I am not an administrator, nor did I ever profess the desire to be one. To quote George C. Scott, who growled in his legendary cinema portrayal of General George Patton, "I am a combat soldier." ⏎

During my educational career, all I wanted to do was teach kids. THEY, and they alone, were my focus. Sure, I performed all the other tasks, to the best of my ability, that a teacher is required to do in modern America. I worked with my fellow faculty and administrators. I was active in the union. I adapted to the absurd directives of the politicians, perpetually maintaining a positive demeanor when engaged with the youngsters, even while seething to a boil due to the idiocy emanating from Albany and Washington.

What I am trying to accomplish with this piece is to bottle the essence of what went on between me and the children. Everyone who set foot in my room can agree that what we did was not perfect. On the contrary. But it was MAGICAL.

Abracadabra.

THE FIRST DAY OF SCHOOL

I entered my first day of middle school scared and intimidated. Especially knowing that I was going to be in an advanced math class. I was never as nervous about anything in my life as I was walking into Mr. Fiore's classroom. The rest of my classmates were most likely just as nervous as I was. Maybe after only ten minutes of getting to know Mr. Peter Fiore, we weren't nervous anymore, we weren't scared. He was calm, kind, and funny. He was also serious, serious about his curriculum. I think Mr. Fiore became the reason I love math so much. Sitting in his classroom every day for two years was an incredible opportunity, and I wouldn't trade it for the world. – Alexis L., student, 2009-2011

Like the old saying goes, you only have one chance to make a first impression. It only took me a couple of years at the very beginning of my career to realize the overwhelming significance of the following statement.

THE FIRST DAY OF SCHOOL IS THE MOST CRITICAL DAY OF THE TEACHER'S CALENDAR. Period.

Remember this, young instructors, even if you forget everything else from this publication: on Day #1, the students are more afraid of you than you are of them. Use that anxiety to your advantage, and you shall set the tone for the rest of the school year. I unequivocally guarantee it.

On Day One, like every other day thereafter, I would be out in the hall monitoring the corridor while simultaneously greeting my kids as they entered the classroom. Not knowing any better, the students would take whatever seats they liked, friends grouped together. When the bell rang, I would walk in, introduce myself, and quietly ask them to stand up and ring themselves around the perimeter of the desk area.

My initial arrangement had the students seated alphabetically, and my reasons were logical. I wanted to know their names, and the best method for me to do so was to group them in this fashion. When I read each student's name, after they were seated, I would ask them if I had pronounced it correctly. With a highly diverse ethnic population, in many cases my request was a necessity. As each child was placed, I would begin to associate the name with the face.

I gave myself a serious challenge each year to memorize all my students' names after only one day in my classroom. On the second day, the very first thing I would do is rattle off each of their names. Invariably, I would get them all correct, and their faces would show utter amazement. Then I would say, "Why did I just do this? By the way, it wasn't to show off." No one, of course, would answer. Then I would provide it.

"Because you are important to me." And I'd have them, for the year.

Honestly, I also did this to show off, a little. ▯

I was a mathematics teacher, and the first day's lesson would have absolutely nothing to do with math. Maybe even the second day's as well. After all, before we begin to learn the math, we need to begin to learn how to learn.

Throughout one's life in school, you always have a favorite teacher. As all my years in school went by my favorite usually changed, until I entered the 7th grade. When I first met Mr. Peter Fiore, I'm not going to lie, I was intimidated. It was my first year in an advanced math class and I was a little scared. I didn't really know what to expect. But after the first couple of weeks of school I wasn't scared anymore. – Alexis L., student, 2009-2011

Back to Opening Day, once the students were seated alphabetically, I would explain the rules of the classroom, and there were only two. I'm dead serious.

Rule #1: No dissing. Short, sweet, and widely encompassing. We will not disrespect each other, verbally or physically. You will most certainly not disrespect me, and I will in return most certainly not disrespect you. We will show respect toward the physical environment of the classroom, keeping our work areas neat and placing your desks and chairs in the correct positions before you leave. You will demonstrate respect to all adults in the building. And, most importantly, you will not diss yourself, in any way, shape or form. Ever.

Rule #2: We watch each other's backs, AT ALL TIMES. This second regulation also came with broad implications. We help each other in the classroom with the math. We are there for each other when personal problems occur, and they ARE going to occur. We remind each other of the proper way to behave, inside and outside the classroom and school. We understand that sometimes life brings us difficulties, and people need their space.

That was all. No page after page of class rules, expectations, course outlines, homework policies, testing procedures. No, not on the first day. I mean, we are dealing here with early teenagers who are going to have an impossible time remembering their locker combination. Thus, I felt swamping them with regs would just further confuse a bunch of already discombobulated minds.

Instead, I was going to project a simple, consistent message. I am a firm believer that too many rules result in too many things to forget. My kids had enough on their plates. They were entering their teen years, and the hormones were racing. The 7th graders were new to the building, away from the cozy environs of elementary school. Some of my 8th graders, the advanced ones, were taking a high school course, either Integrated Algebra or Algebra I. In either case, what they required was Simplicity of Steel. I am from Lackawanna, after all.

No, sir. Keep it simple and remind them every day. They'll remember soon enough.

Oh, and one more thing (channeling Lt. Colombo). I made it a point to let them know, in as direct a presentation as possible, that everyone succeeds. Many of them, especially those who historically had trouble with math, would just stare back with a blatant "Yeah, sure" expression on their face. But I meant what I said.

EVERYONE SUCCEEDS.

WHO IS THIS TEACHER?

That one teacher.... It's been over a decade since the first time I stepped foot into Mr. Ficre's classroom. 11 years... yet I still remember so much... may not remember all the math I learned those two years.... but I remember the energy that radiated off Mr. Fiore's smile. I remember how dedicated he was to his students. Math wasn't my favorite subject until I was in Mr. Fiore's class. I remember him showing us his alumni walls plastered with former students and pulling out our attendance sheet, telling us how he took it upon himself to remember every one of us. I remember him telling us that he refuses to be like the teachers "over there", who won't even remember our names, or take the time to help us fully understand something... and he was right... they didn't. Throughout the rest of my high school years, no one quite matched his love and dedication to his students. I remember him showing us the Buffalo Bills art that hung on his front wall...if I'm recalling correctly... he made it out of yarn...oh! and how we were forbidden of mentioning the you know who's (Miami Dolphins hee hee). Anyways, nostalgic memories aside... now I am on my own path to becoming a teacher.... and whenever the topic of becoming a teacher comes up, I always must talk about that ONE TEACHER.... "you know the more I learn about the art of teaching...the more I realize what crappy teachers we had growing up.....but you know what, I had that one teacher... Mr. Fiore... he was amazing....he was my middle school math teacher. He always took the time to help me understand...even if it meant coming back to him from the "other side". He would use HIS free time to help us. Sure, there were some wonderful... nice teachers...but not like this guy... this guy loved what he did. He genuinely loved his students....and his students felt that. Kids just know...they feel it in their heart who cares about their future and who's merely there for a paycheck. He came to work and put in 110%! He made sure we all put in 110%..." So, when my cousin was in middle school and came and told me, "I saw your picture on the wall in class." And I said, "No way you have Mr. Fiore?!!" She said, "No, he retired." I said "Well... you really missed out on a great teacher." He may be retired, but now his legacy runs in the blood of his students who are becoming teachers and doctors and engineers. I cannot wait to read his book and have yet another lesson from the greatest teacher known to Lackawanna. I'll probably be sitting on the couch soaking in every word with little me hearing his voice thru the pages... taking me back to my 7th grade homeroom... As I continue to learn about differentiated instruction and all the different learning theories... I remind myself of the power and impact a great teacher holds in the lives of their students... and that's not something you're taught through the textbooks...it is something you're taught through example. And no matter the amount of years that pass since I last sat in his class... every day I will strive to become even half of the teacher he was. Because one day I want to be that one teacher... – Nora B., student, 2006-2008

The impact of a teacher on a child is virtually incalculable, and it may take years for a former student to truly realize the effect of the association. Sadly, some students are never reached but, like shooting a score of 18 on a regular golf course, a complete impossibility, you still must try. One of the things I always strived for each day I was in front of kids was to follow the mantra of my old baseball pitching days: ALWAYS BRING THE HEAT.

What do I mean by this? Well, my mind set was that, during a typical class period, I had 42 minutes to teach a lesson, instruct in an engaging fashion, have the lesson accepted and understood by young minds through which hormones are raging like the legendary Johnstown flood, and all the while maintain order and proper decorum. To say the least, it was a daunting task, yet I managed to pull it off, at least on most days.

Let's do some math. In New York State, a school year lasts 180 days. With a normal class of 42 minutes, that's 7,560 minutes per year. Or 126 hours. Or 5.25 days. That means that each parent who entrusted me to instruct their child allowed me to have them in my sole custody for five-and-one-quarter full 24-days of the youngster's highly impressionable life. Do you think there is adequate time to make a difference now?

Mr. Fiore is more than an incredible teacher, although he certainly is one. He is an amazing person who cares deeply about every one of his students. I had him as a teacher when I was in seventh grade, and almost five years later, his many valuable lessons continue to influence me. He taught me not only about math, but about life. He is kind, brilliant, and without a doubt the best teacher Lackawanna has ever had the honor of having in their system. I can't thank him enough for everything he's done for me over the years. – Bailey B., student, 2013-2014

One of the things I learned during my evolution as a teacher was that I should never fail to demonstrate my humanity, and thus my fallibility. We are all imperfect beings, and if we neglect to recognize that fact, we are doomed as educators. Some of the most effective, and most humorous times, I had in the classroom were circumstances in which I somehow screwed up, either presenting a lesson, or perhaps in my mode of attire.

Once I came to work with a black shoe on my left foot, and a brown shoe on my right. Seriously. To compound the matter, the black was a slip-on, while the brown was laced. Yes, it was a rough morning. Anyway, one of my sharp young ladies noticed this at the beginning of first period, and all I could do was laugh it off along with the rest of the kids. So, I did and, if I recall correctly, the lesson of the day went swimmingly. Suffice to say, I spent all my free time in my room, with the door closed. Fortunately, I had brought my lunch.

TRAUMA TURNS TO TRIUMPH

You were hands down the best teacher I have ever had. Not only with math but also with personal problems. You always gave us encouragement. You never gave up on us. I remember how upset you got when we didn't do a good job on the tests. When you would get upset, I used to think it was just a test, why is it that big of a deal? But now I realize you did that because you cared and wanted us to do better. No teacher has ever done that, they just handed back the tests and didn't say anything. But you constantly pushed us to do better. My biggest thing with you was you understood us. You KNEW Lackawanna, you knew where we came from and understood all of us, and that's one of the traits that made you so special. Also, the Wall of Fame! Recognizing students for doing good and keeping them up there even after they've graduated and gone. That to me was very special. And when I was depressed and had things going on, you noticed and pulled me aside and took the time out of your day to make sure I was okay. And to this day I still thank you for that. So as far as the most important characteristics of a teacher to me, I would have to say someone who motivates students to be better, not just in the classroom but also outside life. Someone who shows they care about each individual student, and who has no problem helping a student in need. Tries their best to understand them no matter where they come from. And never gives up on someone. – Cheyenne B., student, 2008-2010

One could say I was born to teach middle school, or at the very least **created**. The two years I spent in junior high (the term for middle school back in the 60's) were, in so many ways, the most significant of my life. To fully understand the personal struggles of that time frame, however, you need to comprehend the background.

I started reading at age three and was able to grasp articles in the newspaper shortly thereafter. By the time I entered Kindergarten, I was already at a fourth-grade level. In my seventh year, I was consuming works on the Civil War and the American Revolution penned for adults. History was, and still is, my favorite subject.

In class, though, I was a behavioral nightmare. The work to me was absurdly simple. I was bored out of my freaking skull and, like any normal 7-year-old confronted with such a scenario, I acted out in frustration. I remember my second-report card from Mrs. Kull's class at McKinley School. Academically, my grades were straight A+ from top to bottom. The conduct page, though, was the total opposite. Nothing but U's for Unsatisfactory. Uh-oh. The powers-that-be in the school did not know how to deal with me. You see, back in those days, there were not programs for "gifted" students, and I had been blessed with an IQ which was documented at the genius level.

Finally, someone came up with a "brilliant" idea. HEY, SEND PETER AHEAD TO 4TH GRADE! He doesn't need to attend 3rd. Let's tear him away from all his friends, kids who he had been with since Kindergarten, and move him into an entirely new group of children, all of whom were at least one year older. What an outstanding solution!

The problem was, nobody asked me how I felt about it. A kid's feelings? Man, this was 1962, and children did what they were told, no questions asked. If they had bothered to inquire, I would have told them an unequivocal "No!" In fact, although nary a soul seemed to care, I was absolutely petrified at the prospect.

So, I skipped a year of school, and my personality changed practically overnight. I became shy and introverted. Simultaneously, my vision deteriorated, and I had to start wearing glasses. With a subdued persona and a pair of those incredibly stylish spectacles of the 1960's, I became in short order the poster child for the University of Dork.

The remainder of my tenure at McKinley School gradually improved, and I made friendships which remain strong to this very day. My grades were, of course, excellent, and I excelled in sports, especially baseball. Life was getting better. Then came the nightmare of Ridge Junior High.

Daily, as the youngest person in the entire building during 7th grade, and the youngest in my level during 8th, I was bullied, harassed, and generally overwhelmed by a new group of students who were bigger, stronger, incredibly ill-tempered, and generally mean. The hallways were a living nightmare. The bus rides to and from school were a sheer torture of coping with non-stop smoking, swearing, and put downs. Even homeroom, where I reported for attendance purposes to start the day for a brief 15-minute period before joining my classmates for the rest of the school session, was virtually unbearable, thanks to one sadist who will remain unnamed.

My only sanctuaries, relatively, were my regular classes, where I was grouped with 29 other "advanced" boys. The other accelerated class consisted solely of girls, but we never intermingled except in the hallways during the school day. In class, I could excel, if not dominate, and get back at those ruffians, some of which unfortunately who were part of the class roster. Every single day, I would kick their asses in Math, Social Studies, English, and Science, evening the score before facing another onslaught of mental and physical anguish before the bell rang.

This was my scholastic life for two years, and the events therein made such an impact that I am still seeking solutions in therapy to the present time. But the traumas transformed to triumph, as they also constructed, as an adult, a damn good middle school instructor, if I may say so.

If there was anything to remember about my experience in middle school, it was having the pleasure of being taught by one of greatest math teachers of all time. I was in Mr. Fiore's 7th and 8th grade math classes, and it changed my life as a student and person. He is a teacher that goes above and beyond the classroom, making sure his students understand the material being taught. Any struggle would result in him staying after to make sure the student understands it. He is not only a teacher, but a leader that inspires his students to achieve the best they can. His work ethic and dedication are unparalleled. If you need someone to talk to, he was there. If you needed help with math, he was there. If you needed advice, he was there. His influence inspired me to achieve great things up to this day in college. He will always continue to achieve great things. I wish you the very best, Mr. Fiore, and I thank you for everything you have done for me. – Joseph K., student, 2007-2009

Never would I allow a student to be abused by another in my presence. My classes were a "safe haven," especially for the smaller, smarter, or less physically fit boys with whom I had a strong connection. Lessons were periods of engagement, where every single youngster was given an opportunity to express themselves without fear of retribution.

No dissing, you see.

And, if a student tested the regulations, and they most certainly would try, they would receive a private conversation from yours truly, and that would be that.

I discovered that one of the best ways to handle a difficult student was to literally stop the lesson when the disruption occurred, take the youngster out into the hallway, close the door behind us, and have a concise one-on-one discussion, with voices barely above a whisper. Admittedly, it helped that I had grown into a very strong individual with a long background in athletics, so my physical presence was utterly evident during the dialogue. Getting my point across took barely a minute or two, and then we both returned to the room to resume our duties. While we were gone, the rest of the students would invariably sit quietly, waiting for us to return. Likely, they were mentally putting themselves into the shoes of their fellow classmate out in the corridor.

As you can probably surmise, I did not have to do this very often.

THE LESSONS MAY NOT BE INTERESTING, WHICH IMPELS YOU TO BE

I had the immense pleasure of having Mr. Fiore as my teacher in 7th and 8th grade, as an advanced math student. To say this man shows talent at his profession, is not only an understatement but perhaps an undermining crime. Never in 23 years have I known an educator with the same passion and devotion to his students that Mr. Fiore exhibits on an everyday basis. He not only has the capacity to drill the subject of math into a students' young minds with impeccable precision, but also could make it enjoyable at the same time. – Petar P., student, 2005-2007

*Mr. Peter Fiore is a six-star teacher on a five-star scale. When I was in grade school, he instructed my Algebra class, but what he taught was far more than Algebra. He taught life. Mr. Fiore understands the differences of each student and will go the extra mile to ensure each child understands the concepts. Beyond that, he knows—and considers—the attention span of children. Throughout class he would pause after a solving a problem and talk to us about a random fact. Whether it was current events, baseball or a fun fact he seemed to pull from thin air, he mesmerized us with a short monologue and then jumped back into the material. It gave us a break and allowed us to focus more when he began our work again. He **easily** beat the fatigue of seventh and eighth graders doing math for long periods of time.* – Hannah G., student, 2007-2009

My teaching career spanned 20 years over a 41-year period. I taught my first five years out of college, left the profession voluntarily to try something else, did a lot of "something else" for the next 21 years, and then returned to the classroom at age 46 for another 15-year session, finally retiring in 2016.

I taught one subject, mathematics, for my entire career. And virtually every lesson I ever instructed centered around the branch of mathematics which has mesmerized young people for generations. We are speaking, of course, of algebra. More times than I could count, I heard the proclamations. "Algebra makes no sense to me." "When will be use this stuff in the real world?" "I can understand numbers, but LETTERS?" "When will be use this in the real world?" (Sorry. This one came up a lot.)

I understood early in my teaching lifetime their fears and concerns, but I still had an obligation to instruct the required curriculum. What do to, then? Finally, I figurec it out. I could control whether the subject was perceived as interesting by my students. Some will love it, but most will not. What I COULD control, however, was myself and my methods of teaching. Thus, I decided that, no matter what the students' feelings were towards algebra, there would be no doubt in their minds that the guy teaching them was a most interesting human being.

In other words, I would get the kids to go with me, and the subject became a mere vehicle of transportation. I must say, the process worked like the proverbial charm.

You prepared us not only for exams, but real-life situations. The life lessons that I learned from you have stuck with me through high school, and now through college. There's not enough time for me to express how appreciative I am to you. The perfect handwriting on a chalkboard, using the Cookie Monster voice when class was difficult so we would laugh, pushing us to do our best and a host of other things that made us breathe easier. – Brittany J., student, 2010-2011

Middle school students are very hard to keep attentive in class, especially in math. Mr. Fiore handled this problem with ease. The amount of enthusiasm that he has about the content was remarkable. He would get excited, then I got excited and the rest of the class followed. He had the class so engaged that at some points I even forgot that I was in school and learning. Mr. Fiore also used a wide range of collaboration by switching up groups and giving us the opportunity to teach one another. We would do think, pair, share and then break into groups of four where we would make sure that all four students in the group were able to understand the steps to take to solve the problems at hand. Another reason why I was always so engaged in Mr. Fiore's class was how he made the content so authentic. I was a baseball player since 7th grade and I remember clearly learning about the Pythagorean Theorem. Mr. Fiore talked about how we could use the distance from home to first and first to second (90 feet) and the formula in order to find the distance that the catcher had to throw the ball in order to get from home to second. This made the concept so easy for me to understand. Mr. Fiore's class had the highest degree of student confidence that I have ever seen, including my *college classes. We began to believe in ourselves because we knew that Mr. Fiore believed in us.* – David R., student, 2006-2008

I learned long ago that the average human brain has an attention span of no more than seven minutes. Compound this with all the internal chemicals coursing through the bodies of early teenagers, and it is easy to understand the difficulty of the task I was assigned to complete. The nice thing was that a normal algebra lesson would take no more than 20 minutes to finalize and, with 42-minute class periods at my disposal, I had time for some strategic diversions.

Humor was a huge factor. I have never met a student who did not want to have fun in a classroom. Every period I had between 20 and 30 middle school kids in a contained environment. Talk about an unrelenting supply of raw material for laughs!

Kids can be funny, too, if you let them. And, young teachers, you sometimes must let them. Of course, we were serious about the lessons. Of course, we had jobs to do regarding mathematics. Of course, we had a curriculum to cover. Of, course, we had to be assessed fairly and with frequency.

But, in Room 203 of Lackawanna Middle School, we had a blast doing it.

Here's an example. Many of my young men excelled in soccer. I made a point of attending as many of the Modified and Junior Varsity games as possible, and I took note when one of my guys scored, because the next day they were going to be saluted.

Before, the class began, I would announce to the students that so-and-so had scored in yesterday's game. Then I would instruct a couple of kids to push out the windows in the back of the room as wide as possible. Simultaneously I opened the door. At the count of three, we would erupt in a crescendo of voices trying to emulate the call of the legendary Argentine soccer announcer, Andreas Cantor.

"GOOOOOOOOOOOOOOOOOOOOOOOOOOOOOOOOOOOOOOOOOOOOOOOOAL!!!"

The walls shook. People in other classes poked their heads out of windows and doorways. In Room 203, everyone was smiling. Heck, they were all BEAMING.

Then we would get to work, in a positive frame of mind, on slope or some other 8th grade mathematical concept. Young teachers, do you think the lesson stuck?

SETTING THE BOUNDARIES

But it wasn't always popcorn and sunshine, not by a long shot.

Hello Mr. Fiore, I do have a story to share...It's from your 7th grade Advanced Math class. I remember this one day you organized a contest the day of the football team's home opener. The rules were "whoever guesses the score of tonight's football game the closest will win $3.00.". So, the whole class wrote their guesses on a small sheet of paper and handed them into you. That same evening, I had gone to the soccer field to play and stayed later than usual. When I got home, I remember being so tired that I went straight to bed with dirty clothes on and everything. The next day I get to school and was sitting in your class excited to hear who won the contest from the day before. I ended up winning the contest with a guess of 28-13 and the actual score of the game being 28-16. I was so pumped that I won. What I didn't realize is that the night before when I got home late from the soccer field, I remembered that I went to bed before doing my math homework! The excitement from winning the contest went away quickly when you asked me to hand-in said homework. Safe to say I was on the receiving end of the "Fiore Fire" that day. You were so disappointed at me that you decided not to award me the money from the contest and gave it to the next closest kid who did their homework the night before. I remember being very upset about the situation, but it honestly taught me an important lesson. It taught me that you'll never be awarded for laziness no matter what. If I would've done my homework the night before I would've won that money and felt amazing about myself and all the kids would have respected me. Instead I was used as an example to the other kids and felt humiliated (rightfully so). I live with those values till this day. – Dabwan H., student, 2004-2005

The premise of my teaching philosophy is uncomplicated, and still holds true today: in order to get the work done, we need to have a good time, and in order to have a good time, we need to get the work done. Rare was the day when we did not accomplish this goal. We did not only get the work done with smiles on out faces, we EXPECTED to do so. Success was a given, and so was laughter.

The results were astounding. My schedule generally consisted of an advanced 7th grade class, an advanced 8th grade class, and three "regular" 8th grade classes, all of which included a smattering of special education students with IEP's, and possibly an assisting instructor. Commonly, on a given test or quiz, every single member of the advanced classes achieved an honors grade, while two-thirds of the kids in the regular classes did likewise. Monday mornings, traditionally the dreariest time of the school week, became the students' favorite, when they would make a mad dash to my room's Honor Board to investigate the results from the previous Friday's assessment. The smiles and expressions of satisfaction from the youngsters were beyond priceless and set the tone for the lessons to come. We had created an avalanche of achievement, and it carried all the way until June, long after the Lackawanna temperatures had become considerably warmer.

Even though we always had a phenomenal time in class, the standards were still at the highest level. Invariably, as I was dealing with early teenagers, sometimes they were not met.

You have influenced all your students in a way most teachers never even try to do. You had a passion for the career that not many people have. You had methods that I've only seen in your classroom. We are now 10 years after when I was in your classroom and I still remember the time you threw that crate of folders across the classroom because we didn't do good enough on a test and you felt it was your fault. – Cameron C., student, 2006-2007

Yes, I DID throw a crate of folders across the room. My 8th advanced kids had just bombed a test and I was, uh, somewhat disappointed. Fortunately, I had a huge room with plenty of space, so no one was in the line of fire. Folders and papers went everywhere, and the effect was startling. Genuine fear was observed on many of their faces, and not a one was smiling. Evidently, my performance, calculated though it may have been, had the desired effect. They never tanked a test as a group again.

Mission accomplished.

THE WALL OF FAME

Twelve years ago, I walked into Advanced Placement Mathematics taught by an educator that has always had a respected reputation throughout the school district. That educator was Mr. Peter Fiore. Looking back, walking into Mr. Fiore's class every morning felt as if I was in an entirely different school. Peter Fiore in my opinion, truly represented what it means to "grabbing the brass ring" regarding educational excellence. His dedication, passion, and understanding of teenage students during the transition to into their adolescent years is what set him apart from any educator I have ever witnessed as a student. Pupils of Peter Fiore were always treated as young professionals. He always strived to ensure every person sitting in front of him put their all their effort in to reach their maximum potential in his class. Mr. Fiore was able to find the best in each of us and made sure we knew that we had it. From using motivational tactics such as his iconic Mathematics Wall of Fame, which encouraged all of his students to aim for excellence and in return, we earned a spot and the opportunity to have our legacy cemented in his classroom as a reminder for those who followed for years to come. Peter Fiore took a subject that was extremely dull and mind straining, implied his unique and effective teaching methods and somehow made it creative, intriguing, as well as extremely easy to follow. His fiery passion while educating Mathematics created a sense of enjoyment and interest for the subject that was never there before. Yes, Peter Fiore is an outstanding educator, but that is not what many remember him for. Instead, many remember Peter Fiore as the first genuine life coach to enter their lives at a time when we needed it most. His counsel, words of wisdom, as well his tough love, some way or another has been embedded into the character of almost every person he's ever encountered including myself. I would like to thank him and acknowledge that he has without a doubt cemented his legacy through all us, HIS students. – Sulaiman M., student, 2004-2005

The Wall of Fame.

The trademark display of Room 203 was probably the first thing one noticed upon entering my sanctum sanctorum, and it was absolutely, unequivocally MEANT to be noticed.

The Wall began as a single large foam poster board attached to the chalk board at the front of the classroom, one which was probably in existence from the original construction of the school building way back in 1957. Upon it were pasted on card stock paper the names of the students in large, clear, Lackawanna Steeler blue letters, the class they attended in red, their class average in blue, and their final examination grade in green. Adjacent to each name was a picture of the student, taken straight from the Lackawanna Middle School yearbook

For the kids to qualify for classroom "immortality", they had to achieve (a) a 90% or better average in Mathematics for the entire school year and/or (b) score a 90% or better on the final exam in June.

I think a very important thing a teacher can do to their student is to give them a goal and show them that that goal is achievable if you just apply yourself and ask questions when needed. I love the idea of that Wall you made to show kids that many past students achieved greatness, and everyone has a chance for greatness! Thanks, Mr. Fiore, for being a great teacher! – Adalis D., student, 2008-2009

As one of his former students, I am proud to say that Mr. Fiore has proved time and time again to be one of the best teachers in Lackawanna. Whether a student had an assignment or was preparing for an upcoming test, he would be ready to assist in the best possible way he can. Mr. Fiore understands that every student's path to achievement is unique; some students need more time or less time than others to meet class criteria and appropriate timing to meet their full schedule. That was why he arranged perfect timing and teaching strategies to meet every individual student's academic needs. Just like coaches are always there for players both on and off the field, Mr. Fiore encouraged students to strive for their greatest potential during and out of class. Mr. Fiore actively sought to motivate students to participate in class and help one another through relating to students and providing fatherly-like discipline that affected his students in so many positive ways. Don't just take my word for it. The Wall of Fame in his class which presented a lengthy list of his former students who scored honors in class and/or on the final exam demonstrates Mr. Fiore's years of achievement in the Lackawanna City School District. That is why I am proud to call myself a former student of his class. Thank you for all you've done, Mr. Fiore! – Hussein K., student, 2009-2011

My schedule generally consisted of two Advanced classes, 7th and 8th grade, and three regular level classes, usually 8th grade. Included in those "regular" classes were several students who had special education designations. In many of those groups over the years, I was ably assisted by a Special Education teacher, and to a person they did a magnificent job.

In 2014-2015, I was assigned 5 regular-level 8th grade classes. Thus, without the advanced kids, I decided to amend another criterion for Wall of Fame qualification. Along with the previously mentioned ways to qualify, a student could also reach The Wall by improving their Math average by a MINIMUM of ten points from the previous 7th grade year, so long as they also passed both my course and my exam.

That year, my final at Lackawanna Middle School, 42 students achieved the goal, almost 50% of my total roster, a fantastic performance. And not a single youngster failed the course.

Where to start on Mr. Peter Fiore? This man was the master of efficiently teaching mathematics while making it extremely entertaining. As a nursing student now, almost 14 years later, I still use the mathematical formulas and equations that he taught me in middle school. Not only that, but he cared about us as students. He was there for the good times and the bad times but was always straightforward and honest with his advice. My name still stands proudly on his Wall of Fame and it's a feat that I hold dear. Not for the good grade that I got, but the good times I had in his classroom. If there could only be an infinite number of teachers with half of the expertise and compassion that this man has, school would be considered a pleasure, not a task. Thank you, Mr. Fiore, for always being a class act. – Richard K., student, 2002-2004

Let's start from the beginning! Mr. Fiore and I were acquainted in 7th grade as he was my 7th grade advanced math teacher. From first impressions, I, as an adolescent who was ignorant to obtaining blatant gestures, could sense the passion in him to help and teach students. This passion drove Mr. Fiore to not just teach but connect with his students. Being the educated man that he is, he found ways to get us thick skulled children to understand these levels of math to a greater degree. Mr. Fiore is probably one of greatest resources us students have had. I for one was able to utilize his thirst for learning and teaching up until his retirement! I came to him for help from everything from geometry to pre-calculus. He accepted the challenge of aiding any student, whether he taught them or not, with any level of math so long as they were dedicated. And he honored these dedicated students with his famous "Wall of Fame." I could never come across a student with an unsatisfactory grade! As one of his former students I can speak on the behalf of every one of my classmates that Mr. Fiore was and is one of the best mathematics teachers that we as students had the honor of learning from! – Anthony L., student, 2011-2012

During lessons, I would often notice kids staring at the names and pictures, perhaps dreaming about someday being there themselves. Younger students wanted to emulate older siblings, relatives, or friends, which created additional motivation.

The Wall evolved to become the pre-eminent symbol of my classroom. Fellow teachers expressed their overwhelming approval. Upon initial inspection, our principal, Mr. Jakubowski, cracked that wry little smile of his and said, "Nice, Peter. Nice."

Parents loved the display, and the favorable comments were plentiful on Open House nights. As the years rolled on, The Wall occupied all the space on the sideboard of the classroom, and I was forced to hang the older classes from the soffit on the window side. In time, the room resembled a sports arena with championship banners hanging from the rafters. The posters would even move a little bit with the wind when I cracked the windows open during the warm weather months, creating a kinetic but calming effect.

At the end of the year, those of us who produced the grades we strived for were cemented into the "Wall of Fame" that lined the perimeter of the classroom. The Wall of Fame was a collection of all the students who received grades of mastery on either their overall averages for all quarters and/or a mastery level grade on the Regents examination. This was the ultimate form of motivation that made all of Mr. Fiore's students strive to do their best. I saw the command that Mr. Fiore had over the class firsthand. He was the perfect combination of strict and friendly which made me want to succeed not only for myself, but to make him proud as well. To this day I remember all that Mr. Fiore did in his classes and I one day aspire to be just as good as him. Since this class, I started concentrating on a career to become a Math teacher just like the man that I wished I could be just like. Mr. Fiore is not just an educator; he is an idol of mine and a role model as well. – David R., student, 2006-2008

Education is an extremely important part of life. Without it you won't get very far. For some people learning may not be the easiest task. However, that feat can easily be conquered with just a little bit of compassion. A teacher that tries to connect with students and genuinely cares about their progress in the class, as well as their progression as human beings, is a teacher anyone can learn from. Mr. Fiore is a teacher that exemplifies those core values. In the two years that I was lucky to be instructed by him I learned more than I ever did about algebra and about myself. Compassion, courtesy, and respect were all basic principles taught to us every day. He instilled values and confidence in everyone that sat in his class. His famous "Wall of Fame" that students with high averages made it on, made students feel good about themselves. Most of his students made it on that Wall because most of them had outstanding averages. If there was ever an issue, such as someone not quite grasping a certain topic, he would go out of his way to make sure that student got the help that they needed. Math was never my favorite subject, but Mr. Fiore somehow made it fun by incorporating fun into our curriculum. He did that by having us play Jeopardy somedays and by ways of a multitude of other fun learning techniques. What made Mr. Fiore such an outstanding instructor was not his ability to teach, but his compassion that still shines bright in my memory. Mr. Fiore is a teacher that all teachers can learn something from. – Ariel T., student, 2009-2011

In the years from 2002-2016, students received Wall of Fame endowments on no less than 593 occurrences, with a substantial number of children achieving the honor twice or even three times.

Did I mention that I had great kids? No?

Well, I did. The best, in fact. I wouldn't have traded them for anyone.

THE PURPOSE OF POSITIVE REINFORCEMENT

I believe we should change the way our education system is run. More like improvements and not changes. One, we need to encourage students to have a growth mindset and not a fixed mindset when it comes to education and achieving their goals. I've talked to many students who feel that their grades make them feel like a failure and that the education system only gives them so many chances to get back up and try again. The moment they fail, they feel limited in their abilities and they don't have the value that it's okay to fail and learn from those mistakes. You'd think this is well known by now, but unfortunately with my experience with other students, it doesn't feel that way. In addition to your comment about what characteristics of a teacher are of most important, I would say is illuminating your passion of what you teach to your students in a way where they are all engaged. A great teacher is one who implements real life situations and real scenarios, both good and bad to show how their teaching is applied and what makes it unique. With me for example, I never understood the concept of why we need to take years of math through high school and more in college, before I was a student of yours. Then after taking math class with you, math became a way of life, through great teachers like you and Mr. (Greg) Opalinski in regards to math, I learned that the concepts learned in math class are alive all around us, from the beat of our pumping hearts, the music we listen too, infrastructures, and etc. it was thanks to great mentors like you that brought on that spark that school isn't just homework and grades, but a way for us students to see life differently, in a perspective where math, science, and art are all intertwined in life even to the molecular level. This has become such a passion and interest of mind, that I have taken it upon myself to tutor and mentor high school students and help them understand what they are being taught and how it is all the basic foundation to all the things they will experience in life, whether it be in medicine, engineering, law, etc. being engaged and showing mercy really connects students to their teachers. – Abdulelah A., student, 2012-2013

The world is changing, and so are the people who populate it. Those teachers who fail to recognize this phenomenon are as dead in the water as the Titanic. One of the best conclusions I was able to draw from the rare perspective of experiencing a 21-year gap in my educational career is that the well-worn axiom of "Spare the rod, spoil the child" is deceased, and thankfully so.

I believe the purpose of teaching is to show the kids what to do, not what not to do. Better than show them, GUIDE them, like a Captain navigating a ship (hopefully not the Titanic). Children want to learn and, in fact, NEED to learn, and you as the teacher have the priceless opportunity to become part of that dynamic. After a parent, there is no greater calling in the history of humanity.

I have never met a student who did not want to succeed but, like all of us, each child is a product of his/her past, and negative experiences in the classroom sadly create in so many kids an unbearable sense of failure, some of which are exceedingly difficult to overcome. Far too often I heard the declaration "I was never good in Math" from a troubled student, and each time I would ask myself the obvious question, "How the hell did rational adults allow this to happen?"

Our job as teachers, ladies and gentlemen, is to make sure that the children are taught, that they get it, and not some of them, but ALL of them. To quote the American educational catch phrase of the first decade of the 21st century, "no child is left behind." Maybe I am some sort of educational trail blazer, but I have had this mindset ever since I first stood in front of a classroom during the Disco Era of the 1970's.

Thinking back on all the lives that Mr. Peter Fiore has touched amazes me. He not only was a great teacher, coach and role model, but a genuine person. Currently most institutions take a "person center" approach. Mr. Fiore had that technique many years ago, but it wasn't called that. He had a way of connecting to each of his students as individuals instead of a classroom full of students. He figured out the best way for each of them to understand the concepts in which he wanted to get across. His teaching method had such a positive result that made a student comfortable instead of confused. This resulted in his students wanting to get more and more out of the classes he taught. Mr. Fiore was truly a pioneer of teaching & molding young students who may have struggled and turned them into successful students who received the most that school system had to offer. – Kevin B., student, 1978-1979

Success breeds more success and, after a while, the ability to achieve becomes commonplace and expected. Everyone wants to make the Honor Roll, and most of them do. In my regular-level classrooms over the years, it was more likely that at least two-thirds of the youngsters had honors grades than not, and the advanced classes would virtually be unanimous. People, many of them fellow teachers, would shake their heads in amazement when I posted the quarterly honors grades outside my classroom door. In honor of my favorite baseball team, I would label these magnificent students as my "Math Giants." After all, isn't that the goal?

I led the school in pizza parties, by the way, and each one of them was EARNED. Students of other teachers would continuously attempt to crash the festivities, and they would always be refused entrance, as I believed that boundaries needed to be established and maintained. It wasn't too long afterward, however, that other instructors began following the pattern of Room 203, and the vibe of the school rapidly improved. Pizza and wings, after all, are prime motivators in Western New York.

One of your best characteristics was being down to earth. On the same level, not acting as if you're above, as to not making the student feel belittled. Also being able to teach the WHY of the concept, I personally understand and retain the info better when I understand the WHY, the cause and effect, not just being told it's this and no other explanation. Also, what I think set you apart from many other teachers was the focus on the positive, when we did well, we made the Wall. Positive reinforcement, so many teachers focus on the negative, bad grades, only made a "big deal" when we were too talkative, gave out punishments, took "rewards" away... Instead you made sure to congratulate us on another 100 or passing grade, gave no homework when the whole class did exceptional, built us up even when we did well, made yourself available before, after and during school when we did score less than expected or needed extra help, instead of making us feel punished. – Kelsie M., student, 2001-2003

ROTTEN TO THE COMMON CORE

Mr. Fiore was an amazing teacher and I was blessed with the opportunity to be placed in Mr. Fiore's advanced math class way back in middle school. This math program was a new program and it was a learning experience for all of us. To make a long story short, this class took a lot of trial and error for all of us. Early in the year...a lot of the students were struggling with the curriculum of the program and Mr. Fiore recognized the problem and immediately took the initiative to make necessary changes for all of us to understand the material and be successful. In fact, in college, I still preferred using some of his methods over the methods we were taught. He is the only teacher I've ever met that really put his students first and made it his primary goal for us to be successful. He is the only teacher I can honestly say catered to the needs of his students in order to truly see us reach our full potential and always encouraged us to do our best. He would show us several different ways to do something until he found a way that we truly understood. - Melissa W., student, 2001-2002

Where do I begin to explain Mr. Fiore? He was the 8th grade math teacher at Lackawanna Middle school and my two boys (Shawn and Nicholas) were lucky to have him. Shawn was always very good in math, but Mr. Fiore helped take him to another level and prepare him for high school. Shawn, now 23, still talks about Mr. Fiore and his teaching methods, how when you walked in his class you were a family, how he reached every person in class and how they would have fun but always walked away knowing more than when they walked in. Now Nicholas, 16 and currently a junior, struggled with Math, and it was never his favorite subject until he reached 8th grade. Mr. Fiore taught him in a way he can understand. It was near the start of this whole Common Core switch, which meant re-teaching these students everything they were already taught, but differently, I can't imagine the frustration that both teacher and students felt but Mr. Fiore not only accomplished this, he pushed Nick into making his Wall of Fame (like Shawn did years ago). He always offered extra help whether before or after school depending when was best for students. Nick will also tell you that Mr. Fiore is the teacher that has impacted his life the most thus far. As a parent, I can only say I wish more teachers had his passion. I am thankful that my boys were lucky to have the experience a great teacher. His dedication also went outside of the classroom. He always knew what extracurricular activities his students were involved in and would always support them. – Ann W., parent

I was having a conversation recently with my daughter-in-law, Courtney, a truly incredible woman with an amazing story of her own. She is now a Doctor of Occupational Therapy. We were discussing education and teaching philosophies, especially as related to the Common Core, which her precious three-year-old daughter, Cora, is already encountering in the Montessori school she attends. She asked me what my philosophy of teaching was, especially as related to the new curriculum and methods of instruction.

I replied, "Courtney, I never taught curriculum, I taught KIDS."

Her smile, if plugged in, would have illuminated the entire Pacific Northwest.

For the past five years or so, the insidious words "Common Core" have terrorized the American educational landscape, causing millions of students and parents to suffer previously unattainable levels of anxiety and stress. Parents cannot assist their children with homework, or at least not without enormous difficulty.

Teachers are equally bamboozled, and under enormous pressure to institute the bizarre lessons and methods despite not having the training necessary to properly apply their craft. Chaos reigns, yet the students still must be taught.

It is my firm conviction that the Common Core is one of the most heinous travesties ever imposed on public education. The purpose, its supporters purport, is to better prepare the children for college. My response is, "Why in tarnation is college so necessary, anyway?"

We are a nation in dire need of trades people. Carpenters, electricians, mechanics, welders, plumbers, and so on. Not every child is academically inclined. And yet, this insidious Common Core philosophy, in which every student must comply with strict academic requirements, has simply been created, in my opinion, to continuously feed the college money machine. High tuition. High room and board. Higher student loans. Yes, my friends, it's all about the Benjamins.

Simultaneously, the Common Core has created ungodly angst among the faculties of America. There is simply too much information to digest, let alone instruct to developing young minds. I have a granddaughter, Lia, who is in first grade and has been encountering difficulty in her math lessons. Thus, I have been assisting her of late. At the start of her first tutorial, her Mom gave me Peanut Butter's (yes, that's what I call her) entire math syllabus and supply of workbooks. The stack was 4 inches thick. Just math. First grade. Peanut is 6 years old. Are you freaking kidding me?

Parents all over the country are flummoxed when trying to help their children with homework. "This is not the math I was taught," they cry. The stress is now in the home as well as the classroom. And a vicious cycle is created, one in which nobody wins.

In my opinion, the Common Core was created by "educators" who would not last a single week in any of my old classrooms. Oh, these men and women are smart, all right, but they have no clue how to TEACH. Or, if they ever had practical instructional experience, they completely forgot what it was like. Instead, they sit in their ivory towers and try to solve the American educational crisis by hammering teachers and students in tandem with so much information that all the joy and sense of accomplishment of the learning endeavor is ripped from the classroom, replaced with a pervading miasma of frustration and disillusionment.

No, my fellow Americans, the Common Core has got to go. Like the Ford Edsel of the late 1950's, it has proven to be an experiment gone bad.

KEEP IT SIMPLE, STUPID

Mr. Fiore, the best and most effective math teacher I ever had. After having him for a year math became much simpler to understand and he taught ways to apply it in real world situations. I was more into history before being in his class but after, it became a very useful tool at home and work. For instance, equations and probabilities are very useful to me to learn more about the universe which I more recently have got into. He also gave memorable advice besides just math related. I'll always remember the mnemonic term K.I.S.S. Keep it simple, stupid! Lol. Thank you, MR. FIORE! – Kenny B., student, 2002-2003

When I started 9th grade, I not only hated math, I feared it. I had never quite conquered the concepts and my confidence level was very low. I just wasn't good at it. And then I was put into Mr. Fiore's class. Finally, I had a teacher who made me understand it! He simplified the daunting calculations and taught me to see them in a way that made sense. He was very patient and insistent that I indeed had the brains to handle it. Surprisingly I began to enjoy solving problems. I began to get A's. I ended up getting a 98 on the final and was so mad at myself for missing such an easy question. Easy. A word I had never used to describe math before. But my story doesn't end there. A lot of people complain about algebra stating they will never need it in life. I did. I worked as a pediatric RN in the ICU where I had to calculate dosing based on body weight. Getting those doses inaccurate could have been life threatening. But I did it with confidence and my calculations were accurate. And moving forward...I went back to school to become a nurse practitioner. My first job was with a very stern neurosurgeon. I managed intrathecal pumps for him and had to calculate the appropriate dosing. He told me later that one of the reasons he hired me over the others was my confidence in solving the math problems. I owe Mr. Fiore a big thank you. He is an awesome teacher and helped me more than he knows. – Carolyn D., student, 1979-1980

Teaching can be as complicated as the teacher allows it to be. Basically, I refused to allow it to be so. I geared my lessons, my dialogue, my instruction, my voice cadence, my tone to the kid in the room who was going to have the most trouble grasping the concept. My thinking was, if I could reach him/her, I already have the rest of them. And, again, we all succeed.

Failure was most certainly not an option. Falling back on the second rule of our classroom, we always watched each other's backs. Kids were going to struggle, sometimes with the lesson, sometimes with the situation at home, sometimes with the hormones surging through their changing bodies, or sometimes from lack of food or sleep. Hey, there were times when Mr. Teacher was having a rotten day as well. None of us are machines. We are humans. Thus, we are all fallible. The only way I know to combat that inherent fallibility was to work together. So, we did.

Certainly, for some students, the regular class setting was not enough. No problem. I would see kids for extra help before school, after school, during their study halls, even at lunch time. I cannot tell how often students would bring their lunches to my room, and we would eat together. Sometimes, we would do math after they finished eating, while other times we would just chat about things.

All part of the People Business, my readers.

WHEN DOES THE SCHOOL DAY END?

Mr. Fiore shows an amount of dedication to his work that is unparalleled by any other educator I've been involved with. During the school year he would be in his classroom roughly 45 minutes early every day and usually 45 minutes after school in his room for extra help, on top of the countless hours he spent involved with extracurricular activities. It was during these 45 minutes before school that had the largest impact on my education, even though most of the time the discussion content and experiences were hardly math related. Mr. Fiore would show us his favorite kinds of music, talk about his favorite sports teams, and offer advice to the students around. This taught me two things that have changed my life forever. Firstly, that the Red Hot Chili Peppers are one of the best bands to come about, and "The Lord of the Rings" is both a literary and cinematic masterpiece. Secondly, it taught me how to use my interests and passions to relate to others and develop meaningful relationships. These skills have proved to be invaluable in the professional world and I owe it to him for showing this to me.

The previous paragraph doesn't show how great a teacher Mr. Fiore is, they explain how great a person he is, which in my opinion is the most difficult part of becoming a great teacher. When you take someone that has the personality and character of Mr. Fiore and you couple it with incredible teaching skills, you have created a force to be reckoned with. Over the two years I spent in the Advanced Math class I learned not only to do well on tests and other evaluations, but I learned to understand Math and the underlying concepts. With Mr. Fiore's insistence on perfection I learned to never settle for less, and to NEVER back down from a challenge, whether personal or academic.

I can say with 100% certainty that I still use many techniques that I learned in his advanced math classes in my studies now, as I am a senior in the Mechanical Engineering program at the University at Buffalo. On top of this course of study I am also a Teaching Assistant for Linear Algebra classes here at the University. It is truly an honor to have been one of Mr. Fiore's students, and, in my opinion, it is an opportunity that anyone should try to seize if possible. – Caleb W., student, 2007-2009

To me, the school day never ended, or began, for that matter. The kids were on my mind ALL...THE...TIME. I would constantly work on new ways of instruction. Pairing lessons, small group lessons, large group lessons, peer teaching, poster creation. Sometimes, I asked the students for questions I could place on their tests or quizzes. Anything to keep the class fresh and stimulating.

I also realized that school life also wasn't just about what went on in the classroom. There were athletics to be involved in, as a coach or merely a spectator. Eventually, I became the head statistician and public address announcer for Lackawanna's two marquee sports, football and basketball. Yes, for a considerable time yours truly was the "Voice of the Steelers."

For fifteen years, I was an active member of the Way Off Broadway Players, the astounding ensemble who produced Lackawanna's annual school musical. This participation enabled me to engage young people in a completely different dynamic, and my involvement with the group was one of the most rewarding things I did in my professional life.

Another great way to build a sense of responsibility and commitment is to have a student meet you for extra help BEFORE the school day begins. Some of the best sessions I ever had were early in the morning before the kids arrived for the homeroom period. I cannot quantify the level of satisfaction we both received when the proverbial "Aha!" moment arrived in the child's mind. But I can tell you this: when it happened, the light did not merely shine in the youngster's eyes. It BURNED.

The bottom line is this, teachers. Those of you who hit the parking lot fifteen minutes after the final bell are cheating yourselves and your students of the opportunity of a lifetime. Connect with these beautiful young people. Show them you care. Open their souls as well as their minds. You cannot begin to comprehend the potential each one them contains until you try, and you will wonder in hindsight what took you so long to think this way.

WHAT TO SAY TO KIDS, AND WHAT NEVER TO SAY TO KIDS

1) YES. "How are YOU?" Children need personal connection currently more than ever. Show them that you care about them as people.

2) YES. "You can do this." The kids are looking to you for guidance, for support, for encouragement. You may be the only adult role model in their lives outside of their family. Be their rock.

3) YES. Tell them the truth, and all the time. Today's kids can read through bullshit at warp speed. Honesty is the best course of action, even when there is pain and discomfort involved, be it yours or theirs.

4) NO. "I don't have time to help you now." And you may not, but the student does see it that way. They live in the present. Make the time. After all, why the hell are you there in the first place?

5) NO. Never, ever try to talk the way they talk. They don't want you to be them. They want you to be you.

6) NO. Don't try to be their friend. You are NOT their friend; you are their TEACHER. You are the adult, and they are the children. In time, friendships can, and will, develop, and that is good. But not yet.

20 BULLETS FOR NEW TEACHERS (AND OLD ONES, TOO)

- TALK to your kids. They are people, too, just younger.

- LISTEN to your kids. Their honesty is as subtle as a left hook to the jaw.

- No matter how much they complain, kids want structure in the classroom. Thus, give them what they want.

- If you are not passionate about what you do, the kids will react in a dispassionate fashion about what you present.

- You are human, and thus will make a ton of mistakes. Don't be afraid to let the children witness your humanity.

- You are there for your students, not the other way around.

- Teach your children, NOT your curriculum.

- This is the 21st century, and the dynamic has changed. If you show the kids respect first, they will pay it back, tenfold.

- Set difficult but attainable goals for each student and class, and then immediately reward them when they achieve it.

- Like it or not, you are a role model to impressionable young individuals. Dress and act accordingly.

- Understand that you are, in effect, a farmer, but the seeds you sow may not sprout for years to come.

- Accentuate the positive, not the negative.

- The sounds of classic rock or R&B emanating from your classroom first thing in the morning will produce countless smiles from your kids. Guaranteed. ☺

- The subject you teach may be as boring as hell to the students, which impels you not to be.

- You don't just teach the subject of your choice. You also teach life.

- The school day does not stop with the bell at the end of the final period. Get involved with the kids after school, somehow.

- Teacher consistency leads to greater student performance. I should know, as I wrote my master's project on that very subject, and got an A.

- Encourage classroom visits from former students, even during lessons.

- If you have the gift of voices, use it. Talking like the Cookie Monster was my specialty. ☺

- Tell them you love them as often as necessary. Like, every day.

QUOTES ON TEACHING FROM FAMOUS PEOPLE

The following individuals express aspects of my teaching philosophy as well as I ever could.

The mediocre teacher tells. The good teacher explains. The superior teacher demonstrates. The great teacher inspires. – William Arthur Ward

If a country is to be corruption free and a nation of beautiful minds, I strongly feel there are three key societal members who can make a difference. They are the father, the mother, and the teacher. – A.P.J. Abdul Kalam

A good teacher, like a good entertainer, must first hold his audience's attention. Then he can teach the lesson. – John Henrik Clarke

Success is a lousy teacher. It reduces smart people into thinking they can't lose. – Bill Gates

A good teacher must be able to put himself in the place of those who find learning hard. – Eliphas Levi

Experience is a hard teacher because she gives the test first, the lesson afterward. – Vernon Law

Your best teacher is your last mistake. – Ralph Nader

One looks back to the appreciation of the brilliant teachers, but with gratitude to those who touched our human feelings. The curriculum is so much necessary raw material, but warmth is the vital element for the growing plant and for the soul of the child. – Carl Jung

You don't raise children, you raise adults. - Deborah Rexrode Fiore (my wife, who is famous to me.)

Everyone who remembers his own education remembers teachers, not methods or techniques. The teacher is the heart of the educational system. – Sidney Hook

I like a teacher who gives you something to take home to think about besides homework. – Lily Tomlin

I have come to believe that a great teacher is a great artist and that there are as few as there are any other great artists. Teaching might even be the greatest of the arts since the medium is the human mind and spirit. – John Steinbeck

A teacher who is attempting to teach without inspiring the pupil with a desire to learn is hammering on cold iron. – Horace Mann

The greatest sign of success for a teacher...is to be able to say, 'The children are now working as if I did not exist.' – Maria Montessori

I touch the future. I teach. – Christa McAuliffe

There are two kinds of teachers: the kind that fill you with so much quail shot that you can't move, and the kind that just gives you a little prod from behind and you jump to the skies. – Robert Frost

Kids don't remember what you teach them. They remember what you are. – Jim Henson

I never teach my pupils. I only attempt to provide the conditions in which they learn. – Albert Einstein

Teaching is not a lost art, but the regard for it is a lost tradition. – Jacques Barzun

Seek opportunities to show you care. The smallest gestures often make the biggest difference. – John Wooden

The job of an educator is to teach students to see vitality in themselves. – Joseph Campbell

I'm more interested in arousing enthusiasm in kids than in teaching the facts. The facts may change, but the enthusiasm for exploring the world will remain with them the rest of their lives. – Seymour Simon

In a completely rational society, the best of us would be teachers and the rest of us would have to settle for someone else. – Lee Iacocca

The difference between a beginning teacher and an experienced one is that the beginning teacher asks, 'How am I doing?' while the experienced teacher asks, 'How are the children doing?' – Esme Raji Codell

If kids come to us from strong, healthy functioning families, it makes our job easier. If they do not come to us from strong, healthy functioning families, it makes our job more important. – Barbara Colorose

What we want to see is the child in pursuit of knowledge, not knowledge in pursuit of the child. – George Bernard Shaw

The dream begins, most of the time, with a teacher who believes in you, who tugs and pushes you on to the next plateau, sometimes poking you with a sharp stick called truth. – Dan Rather

Teaching is not the filling of a pail, but the lighting of a fire. – William Butler Yeats

Teaching kids to count is fine but teaching them what counts is best. – Bob Talbert

Opportunity is missed by most people because it is dressed in overalls and looks like work. – Thomas Edison

So, what does a good teacher do? Create tension – but just the right amount. – Donald Norman

Teacher have three loves: love of learning, love of learners, and the love of bringing the first two loves together. – Scott Hayden

"'The best thing for being sad," replied Merlin, beginning to puff and blow, "is to learn something. That's the only thing that never fails. You may grow old in your anatomies, you may lie awake at night listening to the disorder in your veins, you may miss your only love, you may see the world about you devastated by evil lunatics, or know your honour trampled in the sewers of baser minds. There is only one thing for it then – to learn. Learn why the world wags and what wags it. That is the only thing which the mind can never exhaust, never alienate, never be tortured by, never fear or distrust, and never dream of regretting. Learning is the

only thing for you. Look what a lot of things there are to learn." – T.H. White, The Once and Future King

I think the big mistake in schools is trying to teach children anything, and by using fear as the basic motivation. Fear of getting failing grades, fear of not staying with your class, etc. Interest can produce learning on a scale compared to fear as a nuclear explosion to a firecracker. – Stanley Kubrick

THE MASTER'S PROJECT

During the spring of 2005, I finally became an official "master" of education, when I completed my masters project at Buffalo State College. Dr. Tom Giambrone, my faculty advisor, was impressed enough that he suggested the paper be submitted for publication, but I was having none of that.

"No, Doc," I said. "Just give me the A so I can get the hell out of here."

The ace was my tenth consecutive in graduate school, and I finished my matriculation at Buff State with an impeccable 4.0 GPA. Hey, I figured if I talked the talk with my Lackawanna kids, I was going to have to walk the walk, too.

I had always believed in the personal characteristic of consistency. Plus, I am a linear guy, albeit with an interesting artistic side. But the systematic approach is dominant, especially when it comes to instructing adolescents. Their minds are all over the lot, and a certain level of consistency is mandatory, in my humble opinion.

The kids appreciated the trait as well. They knew what to expect, and they reveled in the expectation. They understood that they were going to be assessed with a quiz or a test every week, almost exclusively on Fridays. They expected their homework to be checked for completion. They comprehended my standards of discipline and decorum, especially since I presented a role model for them to follow daily.

Without further ado, here are the first two chapters of my work. I apologize in advance for the stilted, academic prose, but one needs to follow the rules of the game, mustn't one?

Models of Consistency:

What Can Teachers Do to Achieve High Expectations in The Classroom?

Submitted for Completion of MS in Multidisciplinary Studies

Buffalo State College

by Peter M. Fiore

CHAPTER I

<u>**Introduction**</u>

In a conversation some time ago with several friends who are involved in education, a question was posed: "What qualities characterized the most memorable teacher you ever had?" The responses naturally varied, yet they all possessed a common theme: whether the teachers were perceived in a positive light ("She literally changed my life for the better.") or a negative perspective ("Man, she was tough, but I sure learned a lot."), the thread of similarity in each answer was the consistency of each teacher's approach to his/her students. The message of the dialogue has since generated a profound effect on this author.

What Do We Mean by Teacher Consistency?

I shall begin by constructing a working definition of teacher consistency. Generally, such teachers possess certain characteristics regardless of their subject area, as summarized by Foote et al. (2000):

> They teach beyond the textbook and teach to the students' current level. In lesson planning they are sure to connect daily teaching activities to the standards and to the curriculum, relate one lesson to the next, and establish clear objectives. They revise lessons often (sometimes during the lesson itself) and keep students active throughout the lessons. They are sure to involve students in establishing rules and consequences. They are professional in dress, speech and attendance. They are professional in dress, speech and attendance. They continuously show professional growth, and model adult-like development. Lastly, they interact professionally with colleagues and administration. (p.24)

Consistent teachers are masters of classroom management. Shores at al. (1993) indicated that a variety of student seating arrangements, ranging from seats in rows to partitioned individual study areas, were needed within a classroom to optimize the positive interactions between students and teachers. Related to effective classroom behavior management is the teacher's use of classroom procedures. "A procedure is simply a method or process for how things are to be done in the classroom." (Wong & Wong, 1991, p. 172) Wong and Wong provided a great deal of information regarding procedural usage in classrooms and stated, "Every time a teacher wants something done, there must be a procedure or set of procedures." (p. 173) Observations revealed that teachers who told students about the procedures in the classroom and modeled and answered questions about the procedures had rooms in which a far greater percentage of students were engaged in lessons and academic tasks. (Emmer et al., 1980)

Consistent teachers are simultaneously intuitive enough to realize that flexibility is essential in the development of their students' academic progress. They must always be aware that there are times when the lack of comprehension by the children lies within themselves. Guskey (2001) states:

If no obvious problems are found in the test items or assessment criteria, teachers must be willing to turn to their *teaching.* If half the students in a class miss a clear, concise question on a concept that was taught, apparently that concept wasn't taught very well. Whatever strategy or examples or explanation was offered, it simply didn't work. When half the students answer incorrectly, it's not a student-learning problem--it's a *teaching* problem. (p 26)

The quality of consistence can be powerfully manifested on an intrinsic level as well. In a seemingly unintentional fashion, teachers can establish many aspects of their classroom's environment, both physical and psychological. Whether intended or not, their consistent actions exemplify ways of doing things. Simultaneously, these same actions will portray values that determine the governance and operation of the classroom, in conjunction with the construction of assumptions concerning the individuals who make up the classroom. (Weist, 1999)

Importance of Teacher Consistency

Teacher consistency is critically important for a few reasons. One is that it provides for the students an opportunity to experience daily an environment in which there are no surprises, that they know exactly what to expect. The students can not only realize a consistent approach in how their teacher relates to them as individuals, but also, they can comprehend an underlying message in the way lessons are presented in class. The converse can lead to poor results and a lack of student motivation. Robert Wolk (2002) wrote about a discussion he had with his grandson, asking of the youngster why so many students don't seem to want to learn the subjects they are taught in school. The grandson replied, "It's like school gets in the way of life." I will attempt to demonstrate that an important aspect of a consistent teacher is to continuously build relevance of the lessons into the everyday fabric of their children's lives.

The consistent teacher is the consummate planner and places a great deal of thought into the actual physical arrangement of his/her classroom. Gunter, Shores, Jack, Rasmussen, and Flowers (1995) indicated that effective classroom arrangement was related to another factor: teacher movement. The proper arrangements not only provide for a variety of instructional activities, but also allow the teacher to move easily about the classroom to enhance interactions with students. Their research supported the positive effects of students' academic engagement and decreased undesirable behaviors when teachers moved about the classroom during instructional activities. This contention is strongly supported by the findings of Welko Tomic (1994):

> Effective teachers prepare with respect to the learning environment well in advance. It is, for example, important to prepare the teaching environment set-up in the classroom in advance. Before the beginning of the school year, the teacher should plan the appropriate placement of the classroom furniture, because this affects the teaching methods and learning activities he/she is intending to use. Appropriate placement makes it possible to shift rapidly between the various teaching methods and activities, allowing the best possible use to be made of the available lesson time. With such a set-up, the teacher can also keep track of the way work is progressing and of the students' behavior. (p.250)

With a variety of environments comes a subliminal pattern of a consistent instructional approach, one which is highly interactive between teacher and students. Though interactive teaching can evolve into many forms, it does involve a consistent set of characteristics, beginning with the presentation and explanation of new subject matter. What follows is a section when questions can be asked, and discussion takes place. The next phase incorporates independent student work under teacher supervision. During this stage, the teacher is moving about the classroom keeping track of what each student is doing, providing feedback, and if necessary, explaining the subject matter once again. (Evertson & Smylie, 1997)

Perceptions of Teacher Consistency: By Teachers

Teachers can be highly critical of each other, and one method by which they have measured effective classroom performance is by determining various levels of consistency in a negative fashion. Poor teachers, they feel, are those who are unprepared for class, lack content knowledge, and do little if any extra research in their field. Passion in the delivery of their lessons is severely lacking or altogether nonexistent. Their method of discipline consists of either yelling constantly at the students or allowing the children to do whatever they like. The ineffective teacher does not possess a clear vision of what the classroom should look like and commits the cardinal sin of a teacher repeatedly: avoidance of the students both in and out of class. (Foote et al., 2000)

A highly emphasized teacher-on-teacher perception refers to how well one is looked upon by peers with respect to classroom discipline. Teachers have a high regard for fellow faculty members who clearly establish and maintain rules of decorum by students. Research findings clearly indicate that the more effective teachers take preventative measures more frequently and keep track of student behavior continuously. They remind the students of the rules and if necessary, explain them once again. (Brophy, 1983) At the beginning of the school year it is important that students are made aware of the behavior expected of them. The same goes for rules and procedures, which must be explained to the students systematically and which they should practice. (Evertson & Emmer, 1982)

By Students

Students approach the notion of teacher consistency from an entirely different perspective. What is most important to them is to learn, and the teacher who consistently allows them the opportunity to do so is the one who will be appreciated forever. The opposite can produce disastrous results. The most common perception of students was that bad teachers lacked presentation skills, their lessons were either too fast or too slow, too easy or too difficult, and provided no active learning on the part of the students. (Foote et al., 2000)

Students welcome consistency in the daily presentation of their lessons, and better results are achieved when they are engaged in a systematic classroom framework. Tomic (1994) elaborates:

The findings of process-product research show that an effective lesson may consist of five sections. In the first place, homework should be discussed, and the material covered should be repeated. Second, new material should be presented and explained. Third, students should be given the opportunity to practice under the supervision of the teacher. Forth, independent work on the part of the students in conducive to achieving the desired learning outcomes. Fifth, process-product research shows that material should be repeated and tested frequently. (p. 253)

Another approach favored by children centers on allowing the students a level of authority in choosing areas of exploration. Topics they find personally interesting can produce engagement in such a way that the children will incorporate better strategies for learning, ultimately resulting in substantial levels of achievement. (Linnebrink & Pintrich, 2002) Of equal importance is how students react to varying degrees of teacher consistency. Hughes and Clavell (1999) cite that students' perceptions of competence, autonomy, and relatedness literally predicted their engagement in school, which in turn determined grades and achievement scores. They also noted that a consistent approach by teachers creates a greater measure of emotional security within their children, and more positive interaction with the teacher and fellow students.

By Pre-Service Teachers

For a professional educator, the initial experience in a non-student classroom role is that of a pre-service teacher, and it is during this term that many of a teacher's values are established. Unfortunately, circumstances have determined that sometimes, in pursuit of a quality evaluation by the supervisory teacher, the pre-service teacher behaves in an inconsistent fashion. Martinez (1998) writes:

> Those of us who have worked with pre-service teachers during their practicum will be familiar with occasions when they have abandoned their own positions on teaching--even those which they can "authorize" with research and theoretical knowledge bases--in their concern to achieve "good" practicum reports, especially in times of teacher oversupply. (p. 265)

Unquestionably scenarios can occur in which there exist grave differences between pre-service and supervising teachers in terms of educational philosophy and psychology. It is critically important to pre-service teachers that their supervisors be consistently flexible and understanding at such times, and that a relationship is established in which both can learn and grow from each other. (Ediger, 1994)

Pre-service teachers are acutely attuned to the characteristics they wish to emulate from their supervisors. The classifications of "effective classroom and behavior manager" and "competent instructor" were each endorsed by one-third of a study's participants as being symbolic of effective teachers. "Ethical" was the next most common description, with slightly less than one-third of the participants selecting this characteristic. Approximately one-fourth of the sample identified traits pertaining to being enthusiastic about teaching. One-fifth of the pre-service teachers cited content knowledge as significant. Finally, "professional" was the theme that received the lowest endorsements, with only 15% of participants referring to this area. (Minor et al., 2002)

By Administrators

Perhaps more than any other aspect of the school hierarchy, the administration, especially the building principal, requires consistency from the faculty. Consistency of instruction, behavior, professionalism, and courtesy are the most important qualities desired by school principals. When such an environment is initiated and encouraged by the administration, the resulting academic achievement will most assuredly be superior. Thus, the obvious question is posed:

how can the school administration create and foster the type of environment which promotes the highest qualities of learning?

One method is for the principal to establish and maintain an effective communication structure with the faculty. Stanley Fish (2001) proposes that this starts with the most basic of premises:

> The golden rule of administration is at once simple and complex, and it comes in three parts. Part one is, always tell the truth. Part two, always tell more of the truth than you must. And part three is, always tell the truth before anyone asks you to. (p. 13)

Through a sound communication network, partnerships between principal and teachers are constructed. The initial step is instigated by the principal who, via conscious effort and modeling of desired qualities, channels his/her desires for the success of the children to the faculty. The goal is to establish the belief in the minds of the teachers that the primary focus of the principal's position is to be the instructional leader of the building. (Maulding & Joachim, 2000) In order to accomplish this task, the principal requires a most significant, unwavering characteristic from each member of the teaching staff: flexibility. A chronic objection of administrators is that their staffs are populated by teachers who are reluctant to change, a cancer which can fester if not treated proactively. A strong and bilateral bridge of communication can eliminate such a problem. (Huntington, 1995)

Principals desire for their teachers to be consistent in a critical aspect of school life, and that is in their relationships with the students. As the leader of the building, the most effective means by which this interaction can be achieved is my becoming the role model for such behavior, a quality clearly noticed by faculty members, according to Harris and Lowrey (2002):

> The teachers noted that principals establish a positive climate on their campuses by treating students fairly and equally...The teachers also pointed out that the principals who take extra time to praise students for their achievements over the intercom, in the newspaper, or with personal notes and e-mails create a positive school climate. (pp. 64-65)

By Parents

The parents are the most important piece of the education puzzle, for without them there are no children to instruct. Sadly, they are also the most ignored and misunderstood. What qualities are important to them, and is teacher consistency a valued commodity? The literature appears to support this contention and places the notion of teacher consistency at the top of the pyramid in one critical aspect: they appreciate and respect the teacher who continuously strives to communicate with them about their child's progress in the classroom.

There are a variety of ways in which this can be accomplished. One obvious solution is to ensure that parents and teacher are *deliberately* brought together as educational partners. In such an arrangement, the power is shared by both parties. (Dodd & Konzal, 2000) An alternative approach is the establishment of an actual written contractual agreement between the parents and teachers. (Coeyman, 1999) A third procedure is to actively involve the parents in school activities, such as interactive homework sessions with the child. (Jacobson, 2002) Lastly, some schools encourage their teachers to visit the parents in the homes to accommodate those who cannot make it to the school for conferences. (Loschert, 2002)

Regardless of the approach of initiating communication, parents overwhelmingly concur that they feel most comfortable with those teachers who express directly to them the notion that they sincerely care about the educational welfare of the child. (Boers, 2002) In doing so, this would help to eliminate the negative feelings that, unfortunately, many teachers have about parents concerning their expertise, judgment, and purposes in the classroom. (Hargreaves, 2001)

This Study

The evidence overwhelmingly supports the contention that teacher consistency is a critical piece of the educational puzzle, taken from the unique perspectives of the teacher, student, pre-service teacher, administrator, and parent. Though different in many ways, all the groups share a common goal, and that is the educational betterment of the child.

Chapter 2 of this study will explore the correlation of consistency with the generation of high expectations in the classroom. Is consistency important in the achievement of such expectations? Why is it important and to what degree? Are there various types of consistency? Are there negative aspects which need to be considered? The pages to follow will address each of these questions.

CHAPTER 2

Introduction

This chapter will extend the boundaries of teacher consistency, demonstrating through the research that a direct relationship exists between the presence of a consistent teacher and the high expectations generated in a classroom. Incorporated within will be the critical component of an interactive environment which creates and enhances an atmosphere of success, in conjunction with the acknowledgement that, due to its artistic and flexible nature, effective teaching can involve an acceptable degree of inconsistency.

Further examination will pinpoint the teacher as the key piece of the successful classroom puzzle, the person who sets the tone, selects the tasks for instruction, and initiates the educational classroom procedures. The chapter will conclude with the ideal scenario of an absolute commitment to excellence by teacher and students, and the achievement of results far surpassing previously attained levels.

Consistency = High Expectations

The equation is quite simple. A consistent teacher will yield high expectations, and from two perspectives: within his/her own mind and those of the children. Oftentimes the germination of a premium expectation level comes as a result of a simple explanation by the teacher at the beginning of the scholastic year, telling the students in so many words that they are not only expected to learn the material, but to excel at such learning. (Berliner, 1983) Research has shown that a major factor in the achievement of high mathematics competency is teacher expectations of the students. Successful teachers *expect* their pupils to succeed, and possess a strong sense of efficacy, in that they feel that they are effective in helping youngsters learn. (Kilpatrick, 2001)

A self-fulfilling prophecy can easily be created by the degree level of the teacher's expectations of students. Overwhelmingly students will tend to give to their teachers as much (or as little) as teachers expect of them. A characteristic shared by a large majority of highly effective teachers is their strict adherence to a set of uniformly high expectations, a refusal to alter their attitude or beliefs for their students, regardless of factors such as the race, ethnicity, or family income level of the children. (Lumsden, 1997)

Consistently Interactive

The interactive teacher by nature is involved consistently with the students. As a builder of minds, the teacher must begin to immediately develop the conceptual thinking skills of the students by means of a variety of interactive teaching techniques. Stein and Carnine (1998) elaborate:

For students to use their background knowledge to solve complex problems or build foundations for later learning, concepts referred to here as "big ideas" must be identified and taught. Big ideas within a content area facilitate the greatest amount of knowledge acquisition in the content area and make it possible for students to learn in the most efficient manner. (p. 228)

The interaction, therefore, does not just involve the teacher and students, but also involves a third component: the subject matter. Effective teaching is a product of the dynamic interactions between the teacher, students, and content. (Kilpatrick, 2001) One essential method by which this interaction yields optimum results is through the proper utilization of *questioning*. Consistently effective questioning is essential to consistently effective teaching. Noted Sandra Feldman (2003), "Teaching is as much about what we ask students as what we tell them." (p. 8) Consequently, inadequate interrogative techniques can produce poor student comprehension. Continuous usage of queries such as "Okay?" and "Are there any questions?" trigger undesired mental responses from the children, according to Simplicio (2002):

No sooner are these words out of the teachers' mouths then students begin to shift focus and attention. In the everyday world of the classroom, when teachers utter this phrase, they are signaling that they are ready to move onto something else. Students have been trained to pick up on this signal. Instead of being an invitation to students to develop insightful questions, these words are often a final curtain call on a current activity. (p. 600)

He further states that if teachers really want to assess what the students understand, they must develop more effective questioning procedures by altering the language that is used. (p. 601)

Success Breeds Expectations of Success

Winners win because they fully expect to win. This credo is applicable to the athletic field, the business world, and the classroom. One of the most important attributes of the consistent teacher is the establishment of an atmosphere of achievement. By tailoring one's lessons to ensure student success, a "snowball" effect of continual positive performance is created. Students should be able to experience success frequently. (Tomic, 1994) In their eyes, the best teachers are those who can instruct them in ways they can learn, along with introducing new concepts and explaining new vocabulary so that the students could understand. (Harmon, 2002)

Many children, especially those who are afflicted with a learning disability, find it difficult to gain even moderate classroom success. Because the consistent teacher is perpetually aware of the critical significance of student achievement, he/she will constantly utilize whatever means necessary to produce a sense of accomplishment with the pupil. One such approach was described by Alsopp, Lovin, Green, and Savage-Davis (2003):

> Because of her concerns about the students' metacognitive deficits, Ms. Dimarco decided to teach them a strategy that they could use to solve algebra story problems. She thought about how she might solve such problems herself, then divided the process into steps. She knew that teaching strategies in the form of mnemonic devices is effective for students with special needs because it helps them to retrieve problem-solving steps from memory independently and efficiently. (p. 310)

The problems faced by special needs children are, in many ways, identical to those encountered by children in general. When children are taught mathematics, for example, by connecting and organizing knowledge, building on prior knowledge, and utilizing the formal instruction of the classroom to subsidize the informal math knowledge of everyday life, success can be reached. Proper instruction of children, especially those with special needs, certainly depends on the capability and flexibility of their teachers. (Kilpatrick, 2001)

Acceptable Inconsistencies

The most important factor for school effectiveness is teacher quality. One of the basic tenets of effective teachers is their unique ability to differentiate instruction to meet the needs of their respective classes. (Glenn, 2001) In this respect, it is allowable for teachers to be inconsistent from one room to the next, as there is no single tried and true instructional method that universally works. Teachers must be willing and able to adapt, most assuredly in the case of special populations. (Johnsen, 2001) Alternative approaches sometimes require examination and implementation, including allowing students the freedom to interact with peers, situations that involve creative thinking, and activities with game-like qualities such as puzzle or brain twisters. (Kilpatrick, 2001) Summarizes Simplicio (2001):

In the end, if teachers are to be effective educators, they must be willing to rethink and revamp their teaching styles in order to provide a more stimulating, challenging, and more exciting environment in which to complete their lesson objectives. (p. 201)

The Teacher is the Key: Setting the Classroom Tone

There are five basic pieces comprising the classroom puzzle: teacher, student, administrator, parent, and (sometimes) pre-service teacher. Though all these components have an impact on the educational levels attained in a room, it stands to reason that the teacher is the key element. The teacher is the individual who, daily, establishes the educational environment of the classroom, and the consistent teacher is one who builds and maintains such a climate at the very beginning of the scholastic year.

Joseph Simplicio (1999) stated that sometimes the most obvious and basic tasks for a teacher are the most overlooked: "As simple as it may seem, the first real step to creating an effective learning environment is the mastering of students' names." (p. 112) The opening day of class, in fact, should preclude any academic activities, and instead must be concerned with the instruction of rules and classroom procedures, and only those which address the students' immediate concerns. Whatever academic tasks are undergone on the first day should be simple and fun, so that the children can experience a degree of initial success. (Feldman, 2002)

The rituals and routines of the classroom not only have to be outlined early by the teacher, but they also must be acknowledged and understood by the student body. One of the primary characteristics of consistent teachers is that they continually engage their students in discussions about various topics, and the best subject to choose for the year's opening dialogue is about the teacher's expectations, the reasons for establishing the classroom's rules, and the outcomes or consequences the children can expect. (Burns, 2003) In doing so, the teacher is exhibiting what has been classified as the most effective of the five different strategies used to maintain classroom order: the authoritarian approach. By utilizing this method, the teacher consistently manages student behavior by enforcing a specific and reasonable (to both teacher and student) set of classroom rules. (Traynor, 2002)

Task Selection: What's Best for the Students

Once the atmosphere in the room has been created, the next major decision for the teacher is evident: the selection of the means by which the students are best suited to assimilate the material. In the course of this choosing, the teacher must be certain to set the bar of accomplishment at an attainable but elevated level. Robert Rosenthal (2002) expressed this train of thought in a rather interesting manner:

> If rats became brighter when expected to, then it would not be far-fetched to think that children might become brighter when expected to by their teachers. (p. 840)

> Presently, there exists an ever-growing body of work supporting the contention that group activities which involve real-life, challenging situations greatly enhance student comprehension. Logically, children are more prone to take an interest in opportunities to learn which strike a chord with their own daily existences. Consequently, continuous incorporation of instructional strategies which can somehow tap into the students' interests have the greatest chance of yielding the superior outcomes which teachers desire. (Gough, 2002)

Simple coverage of curriculum for the sake of coverage does not work, and the teacher who consistently understands this fact is the one who will eventually produce the best results. Today's students will become tomorrow's work force, and the types of situations encountered in the generation to come will be complex by nature with no simple or obvious solutions, as recognized by William

Patterson (2003):

> Teachers who acknowledge that coverage of material neither stimulates
> students or results in much learning need other instructional strategies to
> supplant lectures. One model with which some teachers are finding success
> is *problem-based learning*...In most cases, such problems also tend to be
> interdisciplinary. In a problem-based classroom, covering material takes a
> back seat to assisting students in learning for understanding and becoming
> more self-directed. (p. 569)

The formation of small groups, due to their interactive nature, allows each

student to express his/her ideas and solutions, subsequently making the problem

personally relevant to them as individuals. (Lock & Prigge, 2002)

Plan the Work, Work the Plan

An integral characteristic of a consistent instructor is the ability to plan the

lessons to fit the multiple educational needs of the students. Even the gifted child

requires flexibility in task, along with an appropriate measure of support from

both teacher and classmates. (Diezmann & Wafters, 2000) Such involvement with planning, however, requires time, necessitating a concerted effort on the part of all parties to integrate this mentality into the very nature of the school. Time must be found for teachers to plan *together* and engage in meaningful discussion and analysis, and the potential exists for the very role of the teacher to be significantly altered. (Wolk, 2002)

In all too many circumstances, the best laid plans are led astray, and the teacher is confronted with an immediate dilemma. As previously stated, the consistent teacher is consistently flexible, and this quality is manifested in four distinct ways. The first, *knowing in action*, is concerned with one's ability to respond skillfully and routinely to the unexpected. Second is *reflection in action*, which is the smooth transition during one's teaching when it is discovered that what was planned is needed. Third, *reflection on action*, is conducted after the teaching occurs, as the teacher considers what went well and what requires improvement. Last comes *reflection for action*, analysis and plans to refine or reinforce the lesson just taught during the next class. (Danielson, 2002)

Regardless of the myriad of ways in which a lesson can be taught, the consistent teacher recognizes that the foundation of any successful lesson centers around the three simple tenets of attention, basics, and comprehension. Every class begins with the arousal and maintenance of the students' attention. Lessons are short, pertinent, and the students are continually active, which enhances understanding. (Hurst, 2001) The students themselves are a vital source of planning information, and it is quite beneficial for the teacher to overtly ask the students to identify and specify areas for improvement. (Oppenheimer, 2001)

Expecting to Win: The Teacher Perspective

When all is said and done, the daily classroom dramas are enacted by the teacher and the students. It is through their unique perspectives that the need for consistency becomes not only apparent but clearly necessary. First, we shall explore this avenue through the eyes of the teacher.

Master of Motivation

As a guru of student motivation, it is the teacher's initial function to create interest by the children in what is being taught, and this generation of active student engagement must be continuous. A youngster's experiences in a classroom can be directly tied to the level of interest exhibited, and interest has proven to be a significant predictor of student achievement. (Singh, Granville, & Dika, 2002) One method demonstrated to spark student attention is by means of well-designed inquiry-based activities, which have been shown to be effective in the students' comprehension of content and acquiring process skills. The correct utilization of inquiry-based instruction also allows for differentiated instruction, another component of a successful classroom environment. (Baker, Lang, & Lawson, 2002)

Builder of Value

The motivation of young people is impossible unless two factors are consistently noted: (1) the students are expected by the teacher to learn at a high level and (2) value of the subject matter is created within the students. The children must believe that what they are learning from the teacher is worthwhile and relevant. (Kilpatrick, 2001) The primary goal of the consistent teacher, therefore, is to construct within the minds of each student that the subject being taught has meaning to each of them, as eloquently summarized about mathematics by Gary Stager (2001):

> The most disturbing trend in mathematics education is the banal and trivial goals that have been created for children to attain. Today, we see curricula that are created and implemented based on a single criterion: how well the children score after they are through? Instead, we should begin asking

ourselves: What can we do that will inspire children to love and value mathematics? It is only after we have created a set of tasks that will fulfill this noble and worth mission that we can design a test to determine whether we have succeeded. (p. 64)

Flexibility and Adaptability

Those teachers who have an ongoing desire to be more creative in their classrooms must first admit to themselves a willingness to change their approach to teaching. Never satisfied with the status quo, competent, adaptable teachers understand that past success does not count towards future classes and are constantly exploring alternative methods of instruction which can lead their students to deeper insights. (Simplicio, 2000) Such teachers possess a talent which constantly and naturally occurs, and which can be productively applied in an instant. As Gary Gordon (6/4/02) states: "They keep the best of traditional teaching methods, but constantly add new ideas that help students learn." (p. 1)

Continuous integration of two distinct subjects, such as history and mathematics, can establish a foundation for better comprehension, aids the children in making logical connections, and illuminates within their minds the constant connection between math and the real world. (Wilson & Chauvot, 2000) A competent, smart, effective teacher more than understands that, even though a wide range of teaching techniques may be employed, there will always be someone in the room who "won't get it", that the best laid plans are ripe for adaptation. (Ebeling, 2000)

Cognition by the teacher of the three basic components of *experiential learning* (modeling, collaborating, and simulating) could play a major role in the success of the classroom adaptation process. On one hand, modeling a specific behavior signifies most frequently that the teacher demonstrates for the youngsters a desired skill, which in turn will eventually result in one or more students developing the capacity to model that proficiency for classmates. Collaborating involves the teacher working with one or more students, students with their peers, or even the insertion of an occasional invited guest. Simulating integrates the students' desire for real-life relevance, as the lesson places the skill in a context which mirrors situations the students will experience outside the classroom. (Byerly, 2001)

Rapport with Students

Cites Steve Papesh (2000): "The first lesson involves the fact that, before one can become a good teacher, one must become an interested person. Kids don't care what you know until they know that you care" (p. 29) The consistent teacher is acutely aware of this fact. Far too many students enter today's classrooms from unpredictable home environments, and they desperately need exposure to caring adults who value their presence and who create school settings that are predictable and supportive. (Traynor, 2002)

It is vital that rapport with the students is established early in the scholastic year, and consistently applied throughout the term. Children are highly sensory beings, and they can detect a positive (or negative) impression from an instructor almost immediately. Teachers can construct proper relationships with the children in a variety of ways, as outlined by Thedrick Pigford (2001):

Be warm and friendly and enjoy your relationships with students. Greet them as they enter the classroom and try to say something of a personal nature. Be observant and recognize students who may have problems. Let students know you are there to help. Join in school and community events and take the time to attend activities in which your students are involved. (p. 339)

The goal of the teacher, therefore, is to create an environment, a community, in which the students are anxious to participate on a daily basis, a place where the following thought is pondered perpetually by the teacher: "What is happening in my class today that my students will not want to miss?" (Papesh, 2000)

Captain of a Team

Like the analogy of an athletic organization striving to achieve a league championship, an effective teacher will pattern the classroom as a community of learners with the ultimate prize the complete understanding of the course material. Classes that function as communities encompass four inherent features. First, as previously stated, is the essential belief by all parties that the ideas and methods shared in the room are valued. Second, the students possess autonomy in the selection and sharing of ways to solve problems. Third is an appreciation of the importance of mistakes as opportunities of learning for everyone, including the instructor. Fourth is the recognition that the reason for the correctness of a solution lies in the subject matter itself rather than the teacher's supreme authority or the popularity of the student presenting the argument. (Kilpatrick, 2001)

While all members of the classroom learn and grow, there must be a leader, and the teacher is the logical choice. The great teacher consistently *believes* that his/her approach in guiding decision and behaviors will work, and that a psychological need to assist in the development of young people will be fulfilled. (Gordon, 5/28/02) Starting with the introduction and consistent enforcement of classroom rules, the teacher as captain gradually establishes an environment of mutual care and respect, one which provides the optimum chance for learning to occur. (Geiger, 2000) Contrary to a military captaincy in which orders (lectures) are delivered and expected to be obeyed unquestionably, the effective "captain" of a classroom elicits a barrage of questions to involve the remainder of the community, and individual work is assigned only after the teacher is certain that the children have an adequate grasp of the subject matter. (Reynolds & Muijs, 1999)

The Student Perspective

The consistent teacher acknowledges that all students want to learn and takes the necessary steps to help them attain success. What is important, however, from the students' point of view? Evidence has indicated that there exist dual perspectives which are equally significant to the youngsters: (a) they are presented with a continuous opportunity to learn and (b) they are allowed to fairly and systematically exhibit their knowledge and understanding of the course material through the usage of quality assessment tools.

Achievement Through Practice

Kilpatrick (2001) puts forth a strong argument when he claims, "Opportunity to learn is the single most important predictor of student achievement." (p. 334) Students need to feel that they are being given a proper chance to succeed. This can be accomplished by their receiving a reasonable set of goals and expectations, a continuous stream of reinforcement and praise, a building of a classroom structure by which they are allowed to work among their peers and, most importantly, they are provided with an ample amount of practice work. (Downey, 2000) The students will experience their highest degrees of security when they are able to perform the practice tasks which build upon the prior knowledge they accumulated. While desiring to succeed, the students simultaneously wish to be totally immersed in the activities and stand to benefit the most when the work is appropriately challenging and interesting. (Diezmann & Wafters, 2000) Scaffolding, or the offering of helpful hints by the teacher, is yet another method acceptable to students as a means of preserving task engagement. (Kilpatrick, 2001)

Looking Forward to the Test

When students are constantly presented with their expected level of performance, given the proper instruction, and subsequently provided information about certain qualities of their work and what they can do to improve, the natural culmination results in their actually looking forward to the day when they can demonstrate their knowledge, i.e. the day of the test. (Pellegrino, 2002-03) In other words, "test day" is nothing more than one more day within the regular learning process, especially when the examinations are designed to challenge the students to reflect upon what they have been taught by utilizing higher level critical thinking skills. (Simplicio, 1999)

All students make mistakes, and a constructive method popular with students by which the commission of errors can be turned to the youngsters' advantage is through the utilization of *rewrites*, a process outlined by Michael Perlin (2002):

Rewrites are much more than test corrections. Rewriting is a structured program in which students are given the opportunity to reflect and improve on their original assessments. Students relearn the concepts that were difficult for them to master in the original time frame. They can do this work at school in extra-help sessions with me or with other students. They can also work at home to revisit the troublesome topics with a family member or friend...When they have demonstrated mastery through written explanations and mathematical notation for any concept on the exam, they regain some of the points they lost on their original assessments. (p. 134)

Perlin further states that, for rewrites to be acceptable, students must provide a written explanation of the solution, even if the original question did not require one. The rewrite process also addresses the notion that some students need extra time to master certain concepts. (p. 135)

Conclusion

It has been noted from the literature that consistency is one of the integral characteristics of an effective classroom instructor, and from consistency is derived the necessary ingredients of a successful educational environment: proper class management, thorough planning, flexible and interactive instruction, and the creation of continuous opportunities to learn for the students. A consistent classroom breeds successful student achievement, and the teacher and students are willing members of an exciting and rewarding community of learning. **REFERENCES**

Allsopp, D., Lovin, L., Green, G., & Savage-Davis, E. (2003). Why students with special needs have difficulty learning mathematics and what teachers can do to help. *Mathematics Teaching in the Middle School*, 8(6), 308-314.

Baker, W., Lang, M., & Lawson, A. (2002). Classroom management for successful student inquiry. *Clearing House,* 75(5), 248-252.

Berliner, D. (1983). The executive functions of teaching. *Instructor*, 93(2), 28-33.

Boers, D. (2002). What teachers need of parents. *Education Digest,* 67(8), 37-40.

Brophy, J.A. (1983). Classroom organization and management. *Elementary School Journal,* 83, 265-285.

Burns, M. (2003). The battle for civilized behavior: Let's begin with manners. *Phi Delta Kappan,* 84(7), 546-549.

Byerly, S. (2001). Linking classroom teaching to the real world through experiential instruction. *Phi Delta Kappan,* 82(9), 697-699.

Coeyman, M. (1999, November 2). Schools make a contract--with parents. *Christian Science Monitor*, p. 13.

Danielson, L. (2002). Developing and retaining quality classroom teachers through mentoring. *Clearing House,* 75(4), 183-185.

Diezmann, C. & Wafters, J. (2000). Catering for mathematically gifted elementary students: Learning from challenging tasks. *Gifted Child Today Magazine,* 23(4),14-20.

Dodd, A.W., & Konzal, J.L. (2000). Parents and educators as real partners. *Education Digest,* 65(7), 18-22.

Downey, C. (2000). Top 10 instructional strategies for achievement. *Leadership,* 30(2), 11.

Ebeling, D. (2000). Adapting your teaching to any learning style. *Phi Delta Kappan,* 82(3), 247-248.

Ediger, M. (1994). Problems in supervising student teachers. *Education,* 114(4), 628-630.

Emmer, E., Evertson, C., & Anderson, L. (1980). Effective management at the beginning of the school year. *The Elementary School Journal,* 80, 219-231.

Evertson, C., & Emmer, E. (1982). Effective management at the beginning of the school year in junior high classes. *Journal of Educational Psychology,* 74, 495-498.

Evertson, C.M., & Smylie, M.A. (1987). Research on teaching and classroom procedures. In J.A. Glover & R.R. Running (Eds.), *Historical foundations of educational psychology,* (pp. 349-371). New York: Plenum Press.

Feldman, S. (2002). A good first day. *Teaching PreK-8,* 33(1), 8.

Feldman, S. (2003). The right line of questioning. *Teaching PreK-8*, 33(4), 8.

Fish, S. (2001). To thine own self be truthful. *Chronicle of Higher Education,* 48(8), 13-14.

Foote, C., Vermette, P., Wisniewski, S., Agnello, A., & Pagano, C. (2000). The characteristics of bad high school teachers reveal avoidable behaviors for new teachers. *Education,* 121(1), 15-26.

Geiger, B. (2000). Discipline in k through 8th grade classrooms. *Education,* 121(2), 383-393.

Glenn, R. (2001). What teachers need to be. *Education Digest*, 67(1), 19-21.

Gordon, G. (2002, May 28). Belief in teaching energizes great teachers. *Gallup Poll Tuesday Briefing,* pp. 1-2.

Gordon, G. (2002, June 4). Great teachers are storehouses of information. *Gallup Poll Tuesday Briefing,* pp. 1-2.

Gough, P. (2002). Interest matters. *Phi Delta Kappan,* 83(8), 566-567.

Gunter, P.L., Shores, R.E., Jack, S.L., Rasmussen, S.K., & Flowers, J. (1995). On the move: Using teacher/student proximity to improve students' behaviors. *Teaching Exceptional Children,* 28(1), 12-14.

Guskey, T.R. (2001). Use test results as tools to improve teaching. *Education Digest,* 66(5), 25-28.

Hargreaves, A. (2001). Beyond anxiety and nostalgia. *Phi Delta Kappan,* 82(5), 373-377.

Harmon, D. (2002). They won't teach me. *Roeper Review,* 24(2), 68-75.

Harris, S.L., & Lowrey, S. (2002). A view from the classroom. *Educational Leadership,* 59(8), 64-65.

Hughes, J., & Clavell, T. (1999). Influence of the teacher-student relationship in childhood conduct problems: A prospective study. *Journal of Clinical Child Psychology,* 28(2), 173-184.

Huntington, F. (1995). A simple idea to spark change. *Thrust for Educational Leadership,* 25(2), 26-27.

Hurst, B. (2001). ABC's of content area lesson planning: Attention, basics, and comprehension. *Journal of Adolescent & Adult Literacy,* 44(8), 692-693.

Jacobson, L. (2002). Putting the 'parent piece' in schools. *Education Week,* 22(5), 1-3.

Johnsen, S. (2001). Teachers do make a difference. *Gifted Child Today Magazine,* 24(1), 5.

Kilpatrick, J., Swafford, J. (Ed.), & Lindell, B. (Ed.) (2001). *Adding it up: Helping children learn mathematics.* National Academy Press.

Linnebrink, E., & Pintrich, P. (2002). Motivation as an enabler for academic success. *School Psychology Review,* 31(3), 313-328.

Lock, R. & Prigge, D. (2002). Promote brain-based teaching and learning. *Intervention in School & Clinic,* 37(4), 237-241.

Loschert, K. (2002). Meet the parents. *NEA Today,* 21(2), 26-27.

Lumsden, L. (1997). Expectations for students. *Emergency Librarian,* 25(2), 44-45.

Martinez, K. (1999). Pre-service teachers adrift on a sea of knowledges. *Asia-Pacific Journal of Teacher Education,* 26(2), 97-106.

Maulding, W., & Joachim, P. (2000). When quality really counts. *Contemporary Education,* 71(4), 16-18.

Minor, L., Onwuegbuzie, A., Witcher, A., & James, T. (2002). Pre-service teachers' educational beliefs and their perceptions of characteristics of effective teachers. *Journal of Educational Research,* 96(2), 116-127.

Oppenheimer, R. (2001). Increasing student motivation and facilitating learning. *College Teaching,* 49(3), 96-98.

Papesh, S. (2000). Insights on teaching from on the job. *Education Digest,* 65(7), 28-32.

Patterson, W. (2003). Breaking out of our boxes. *Phi Delta Kappan,* 84(8), 569-574.

Pellegrino, J. (2002-03). Knowing what students know. *Issues in Science & Technology,* 19(2), 48-52.

Perlin, M. (2002). Rewrite to improve. *Mathematics Teaching in The Middle School,* 8(3), 134-138.

Pigford, T. (2001). Improving teacher-student relationships. *Clearing House,* 74(6), 337-339.

Reynolds, D. & Muijs, D. (1999). The effective teaching of mathematics: A review of research. *School Leadership & Management,* 19(3), 273-288.

Rosenthal, R. (2002). Covert communication in classrooms, clinics, courtrooms, and cubicles. *American Psychologist,* 57(11), 839-849.

Shores, R.E., Gunter, P.I., & Jack, S.L. (1993). Classroom management strategies: Are they setting events for coercion? *Behavioral Disorders,* 18, 92-102.

Simplicio, J. (1999). Some simple and yet overlooked common sense tips for a more effective classroom environment. *Journal of Instructional Psychology,* 26(2), 111-115.

Simplicio, J. (2000). Teaching classroom educators how to be more effective and creative teachers. *Education,* 120(4), 675-680.

Simplicio, J. (2001). How to recognize and counteract student inattentiveness in the classroom. *Journal of Instructional Psychology,* 28(3), 199-201.

Simplicio, J. (2002). Miscommunication in the classroom: What teachers say and what teachers really hear. *Education,* 122(3), 599-601.

Singh, K., Granville, M., & Dika, S. (2002). Mathematics and science achievement:Effects of motivation, interest, and academic engagement. *Journal of Educational Research,* 95(6), 323-332.

Stager, G. (2001). Taking stock of math education. *Curriculum Administrator,* 37(4), 63-65.

Stein, M. & Carnine, D. (1998). Direct instruction: Integrating curriculum design and effective teaching practice. *Intervention in School & Clinic,* 33(4), 227-234.

Tomic, W. (1994). Effective teaching practices. *Education,* 115(2), 246-255

Traynor, P. (2002). A scientific evaluation of five different strategies teachers use to maintain order. *Education,* 122(3), 483-510.

Weist, L. (1999). Practicing what they teach: Should teachers "do as they say?" *Clearing House,* 72(5), 264-268.

Wilson, P. & Chauvot, J. (2000). Who? How? What? *Mathematics Teacher,* 93(8), 642-645.

Wolk, R. (2002). Know thy subject. *Teacher Magazine,* 14(3), 4-6.

Wolk, R. (2003). Worlds apart. *Teacher Magazine,* 14(5), 5-7.

Wong, H.K. & Wong, R.T. (1991). *The first days of school: How to be an effective teacher.* Sunnyvale, CA: Harry T. Wong Publications.

TESTIMONIALS AND OTHER WONDERFUL THOUGHTS

This is the final chapter, and it was entirely written by people very special in my life. Every single word is theirs, unedited (except for the editing of 21st century text language and errata of English composition).

By the way, if any of you are skeptical as to whether a teacher can make a positive difference in the life of a young person, you may wish to take heed of the following.

You were more than a teacher for many. You taught us more than just math, you taught us about the power of determination, perseverance, and teamwork. You believe in your students and their potential to be great. You take honor in teaching at LHS. To us, you are a teacher, a friend, and a role model. So, we thank you for everything. Plus, you could tell the difference between my brother and I, and that my friend, takes true skill and dedication. – Abdul A., student, 2005-2007

I'm sad to say that I never had the chance to have Mr. Peter Fiore as a teacher. But as I heard the great comments and recommendations about him, I immediately wanted to get closer with him to see who this great guy is. The way I met Mr. Fiore was checking into the scorer's table for my basketball game. Mr. Fiore looked at me and said," Go out there and do your thing, Abdul." I then took that as a "Wow, the teacher that everyone talks about realized me." Then days after Mr. Fiore caught me walking the halls and pulled me in and started talking to me about sports, which lead to talking about education. I then talked to Mr. Fiore my whole study hall class. I realized how great of a teacher and mentor he is. He is willing to help anybody out in this world no matter who you are. I then started taking time out of my study halls and going to Mr. Fiore and talking to him for the whole period. One thing I wanted to say about him is how great he is helping people understand what they're struggling with. I went from completely not knowing about a topic in math to understanding it very well after spending a period with Mr. Fiore. The guy's an amazing teacher/mentor and all the above. – Abdul A., student

Math has always been a favorite subject of mine because of the teacher that's has been beside me throughout many years I have been in school. Having Peter Fiore for years has been a great experience for me because of how much he has motivated me to do better or to hit a certain goal I wanted to achieve. Knowing that Mr. Fiore would have used most of his time to help his students for whatever reason makes me appreciate him more. Mr. Fiore is well respected in the school and he also gives respect towards others. He is the first teacher I go to if struggling in math and he will find some time for him to help me on whatever I am struggling with. Peter Fiore is a great role model towards many students and very supportive! – Abdulhalim N., student, 2012-2014

I had Mr. Fiore about 15 years ago and I can honestly say he is one of the most memorable teachers I have ever had! I always thought math was a difficult subject until I had him as my teacher. If you didn't understand something, he made sure he explained it and showed you how to do it until you completely understood it. He cares about every single one of his students and goes above and beyond to make sure that his students learn math with ease. He's an enthusiastic teacher and anyone who has had the pleasure of having him as a teacher, like myself, can tell you that he genuinely loves what he does! He truly is the best! – Ahlim O., student, 2003-2004

Math has always been a subject I have struggled in. I have never been able to understand much from my other teachers and as a result my grades suffered, but in my time with Mr. Fiore, I was able to comprehend what was being taught and apply it. In his class my grades were the highest they have ever been, and I still am able to remember everything he taught me. Mr. Fiore is by far one of the best teachers I have ever had the honor of working with. Thank you, Mr. Fiore, for helping me and being able to make me enjoy going to math class. – Ailana O., student, 2012-2013

You have plenty of traits but one of your best traits was that you made sure every student understood what you were teaching. That seems like a simple task but in reality it's not, and if someone failed the exam you would be upset, not because you were mean, but because you wanted everyone to succeed and you felt almost like you were let down. You weren't only just a math teacher; you were also a life mentor and I personally thank you for all that you've done. – Akram A., student, 2005-2007

As much as I hated math and always looked for an excuse to get out of it, I'm glad you kept me and the rest of my class on track and made us do it every day. It helped me better understand it which is amazing since I'm so bad at it usually lol I also liked that on test days after everyone finished was our only free day because we all knew we could pass with flying colors and then get to socialize. I also loved how you explained math, because it was easy to understand which again is awesome because I am terrible at it. – Alaina T., student, 2015-2016

Honestly, Mr. Fiore was THE best Math teacher I've ever had. This gentleman made Math one of my favorite subjects in school throughout my time in 7th grade. Not only was the class great, but it was fun! – Alec S., student, 2012-2013

There are multiple variables that I can use to explain why I respect you as a person and as a teacher.

First was the passion. I recall multiple times when you would bring up the fact that, out of NY school standings, we "are at the lowest standard but can always make it to be the best."

Second, you were the first teacher to approach me as an individual, instead of being a pre-teen that read too many books and was bored with the curriculum. You challenged me! Embracing the fact that comic books were okay, because we both loved Spider-Man. Your name being Peter...

Third, even after I went to high school, I showed you when I got my black belt and got my Eagle Scout. It felt like I was showing my father because you were so receptive and patient. It's like you knew I was going to do anything I put my mind on, but it was seeing that coy little smile of reassurance that made me become proud of myself. Nothing had to be said. It was just that look when I told you.

Fourth, you have a firm handshake. – Alex T., student, 2001-2002

Mr. Fiore was the best teacher I have ever had. He helped me with any problems I had. He was always there if I needed to stay after school for help. He was the nicest teacher ever. And I wish I could have him as a teacher every year!! – Alexander S., student, 2014-2015

Compassion for teaching is fundamental for making an impact on students. Compassion was something you always poured into your teaching, it inspired me to the core...Your teaching enabled me to find the true value of education early on. You inspired me to always try my hardest no matter how difficult the problem was. Your supportiveness allowed me to further my abilities not only within the classroom, but sports as well. I will never forget my experience as your student. Mr. Fiore, you have impacted my life and many others in so many ways. You are one of the handful of teachers I have met throughout my education who see the good and potential in every student, regardless of any other dynamic. You pushed me to be the best version of myself I could be. When I was nervous and afraid to take the Regents Exams, you never gave up on me. You pushed me to strive for excellence, and I did. You are someone I can look back on and think, "He helped mold me into the woman I always wanted to become." Your sense of humor, genuineness, and compassion made a difference in my life, and I always will be grateful for that. — Amanda H., student, 2009-2011

Mr. Fiore was my math teacher in 8th grade. He went above and beyond with his teachings with expanding his classroom time to before and after class to help students if they were struggling. He would come to school early so students could come to the classroom so he could help them with the homework before students would make their way to their homerooms. He is very knowledgeable with the subject matter and is one teacher who strived to have the students understand and succeed as much as possible. — Amanda M., student, 2007-2008

I don't even know where to begin with this because I want it to contain the same passion as Mr. Fiore has for his students. This man is hands down one of the most important and influential teachers of my high school career, which is a lot seeing as how he taught me in 7th and 8th grade. Any time I was struggling with school I would remember his words and faith he had in not only me but all of us. I know I can speak for every student he's ever taught that he made a difference in all our lives and us in his. He truly is an amazing man with an amazing talent and I'm so thankful to have had to opportunity to have him as a teacher not only with math and learning but in life. — Amanda N., student 2005-2007

In life there are responsibilities and consequences. If you ignore one you naturally ignore the other. Middle school is an odd time in any teenager's life as the calls of structure and responsibility are in sight but just past the horizon. A crossing road is formed at that tender age that measures your determination and will to learn. Applying yourself isn't always the easiest in terms of execution, and it is certainly not easy early in life.

"This will be the hardest test of your life. It will be difficult because you are testing the unknown." I'm not sure if that's the exact quote from you, but it certainly surmises the point. In hindsight it was a simple Algebra I exam that we were preparing for; however, it ultimately laid the foundation on how I viewed the rest of my academic career. As an instructor, you never held our hands. You set goals when we weren't sure of the goals we should set, and you pushed us when we didn't want to be pushed. Although sometimes it seemed aggressive (my main concern at the time was going home and playing video games), your approach on teaching was appropriate. At the end of the day, you demanded results. You demanded more for us as students than we could possibly imagine.

Fast forward ten years after the fact. I am now a man with a budding career and a promising future. THANK YOU for the tough love. THANK YOU for the encouragement. THANK YOU for the disappointment when we as students did not live up to your standard. THANK YOU for the "in your face, now what are you going to do about it" attitude. I hold myself to a standard as an adult I know I will never reach. I do that because I constantly reach for a goal. I want to be a better person than yesterday, last week, and last year. I'm always reaching for more and for that, I THANK YOU. – Andrew L., student, 2008-2010

To me, the best characteristics for a teacher of any subject should be friendliness and congeniality; a good communicator; kindness; a good listener; and, a great sense of humor. You, Mr. Fiore, demonstrated all of them. Your teaching methods helped shape me into the student I am today. – Andrew S., student, 2013-2014

Sir, as a student, the first thing I notice is whether the teacher/professor/mentor takes an interest in you, both as a person and a student. Nothing can demotivate someone more than being lectured without a purpose or a reason. In your class, the "why" was just as important than the "how." You took an interest in every one of your students and it showed during instruction. One other important item is consistent standards across the board. All the good teachers that I've had set standards and enforced them. This didn't mean they weren't flexible, but there had to be a good reason for why an assignment wasn't turned in. A teacher that lets things slide, lets standards erode over time and it reflects noticeably in the class performance. You always upheld those standards and the years of high performers on the boards around the classroom showed that. As a Division Officer in the US Navy, I have to mentor, train, and instruct people younger and older than me. The military is an inherently dangerous job. The lessons I've learned from teachers, such as yourself, have provided me with irreplaceable experience and insight. I like to boil it down to three things: 1. Set, maintain, and enforce standards, but understand that human beings are fallible. 2. Take a genuine interest in people. 3. Think about what it would be like if you were in their shoes. – Andrew S., student, 2008-2010

During my lifetime I have had approximately 60 teachers. I will not lie to you and say I can remember each one of those 60 teachers. However, I do remember quite a few, some for good reason and some for unfavorably reasons. You, Mr. Fiore I remember for good reasons. The teachers I remember for good are those that were relatable. Those teachers that I truly felt I could talk to. Those that held real conversations with their students. Those willing to have a healthy debate with their students. You are all these things. You are one of the reasons I wanted to become a teacher myself. I instead became a mother; I now homeschool my own children. Watching them learn and grow is the most fulfilling and draining thing I have ever done, and I love every second of it. Unfortunately, there are not as many teachers like you. There are teachers who are robotic or disconnected. There are teachers who feel their way is the only way, which is completely the opposite of what children want to hear. As a student I felt that if I had something to say my voice would be heard and accepted in your class. Thank you for being an amazing teacher back then and still now. – Angelina R., student, 2001-2002

As a student, an important characteristic of a teacher was recognizing their students background. I believe in order to teach you must first learn about the individual. Know that we all don't grow up in similar household of co-parenting which often leaves us with pressure of helping to provide for our families in the short term instead of applying ourselves to gain knowledge that can help provide our family in the long term. Some of us may require more attention because we don't have a figure pushing us to our full potential and that is where I believe our teachers come in. A teacher who believes we can achieve and not just saying it can be sensed. A teacher who cares. A teacher who walks out of the classroom in disappointment for a moment because how dare you, Anthony, not apply yourself to study for that test because he or she knows I am capable. To know the teacher cares will set a fire under a student to become better. Not just for themselves but because they know it made that teacher proud. The teacher who is viewed as their figure. Learning about your student and caring are two of the most important characteristics I believe a teacher could have and I believe you, Mr. Fiore, had that. – Anthony R., student, 2002-2003

Well, to start, your capabilities of teaching are astounding. You are considered #1 inside or outside the classroom. I am so thankful that I got to have you as a teacher. You always took the right steps in teaching the material. You made learning Math way easier for me. I can't thank you enough for your enthusiastic attitude in teaching. You truly are a wizard at what you do for us. – Anthony R., student, 2014-2015

Mr. Fiore is one of my favorite teachers ever. Even though he was a math teacher he taught us real world situations. He taught us with respect. I have so many memories in his classroom. Recently when he retired, I got so upset because others will not get the pleasure to be taught by him. He cared about each student that he taught. Besides being a teacher, he did many activities outside the school including, announcing at school games, chaperoning at dances and starring in the plays. He was always after school if students needed help with homework or didn't understand the lesson. Mr. Fiore helped everyone and didn't care who it was. At the end of the quarter he paid for his students to have a pizza party. It was the best to have a teacher care about the students to pay for pizza and wings. It was an honor for me to be a student of Mr. Fiore. – Ariana R., student, 2014-2015

The best education I have had were from a few teachers (including you) that take the time to help you understand. Patience is very important because when I don't understand something, I need a teacher that is not going to get easily frustrated trying to explain it to me. When a teacher seems like I am bothering them when I need help makes me not ever want to ask for help again. One of my professors in respiratory therapy school was so amazing. He was always going above and beyond to help me learn and he was so enthusiastic about his job that made me be more interested the topics. When someone is passionate about what they are teaching you can tell. – Ashley H., student, 2001-2002

As a former student of Mr. Fiore, I can attest to his ability to make any student understand and enjoy math. Math was never my favorite subject, but Mr. Fiore made math simple and easy for me. He has a unique approach that makes learning fun and easy. Mr. Fiore possesses the ability to help any child learn math because he is dedicated to teaching and has devoted many years of doing just that to children in his hometown! There is no one better qualified to help your child than Mr. Fiore!! – Ashley M., student, 2002-2003

Mr. Fiore was one of the best teachers I ever had in math. Not only did he teach us our math, but he taught us to be respectful young adults. He was one of the teachers who cared about his students and wasn't only there to collect a paycheck. He encouraged us to learn and ask questions if we did not understand. I remember when I was in 8th grade and I was having difficulty in math. Mr. Fiore did not let me fall behind. He stayed after school hours with me to explain in further details to help me understand. If I didn't understand Explanation A, he would approach the question in a different way. He would give me math questions to try on my own to see if I would be able to complete them successfully. Mr. Fiore never gave up on us, even when we disappointed him (with our behavior in class or our test scores). He always made classroom learning fun. I am thankful to Mr.

Fiore for being our teacher, and he is one of the best. I looked up to him as a teacher but also as a role model of how a person can add value to other people's lives. Mr. Fiore is a man of character, values, and integrity. – Ashley W., student, 2005-2007

During my time as a student in the Lackawanna City School district, I have encountered some truly incredible teachers. Each of the people who I consider to be an exceptional educator share a common trait: they value life experience above the rigidity of a typical classroom curriculum. This isn't to say that they failed to teach the necessary material; only that they also allowed for ample time to get to know their students as individuals, share stories and ideas, and give us valuable advice. They allowed their students to see them not only as teachers, but as people, and took the time to show us that, though important, there are more vital aspects to life than straight A's and perfect test scores. Though I have only had a handful of teachers like this, the impact they have made on my own life and the lives of their other students is tremendous. These are the teachers who inspired me to pursue teaching as a career myself, and I hope that someday I can encourage my own students the way they encouraged me. – Bailey B., student, 2013-2014

You elevated me from your basic algebra class to Math 9R in the middle of the year. I didn't think I was up to it, but you did. I ended up getting 100% on the final exam. Thank you for recognizing a student who needed a challenge and giving him the tools to be successful. – Bob J., student, 1979-1980

Mr. Fiore, you will stick in my head as not only one of my favorite math teachers but also one of the best. In my middle school career as a student, I remember having you for home room in your advanced math and you single handedly prepared all of us for the upcoming exam. Inspired by all the names on the Wall of the kids that had taken the exam before me, I passed with flying colors and my heart scared when I saw my name on the Wall for the first time. You are an amazing teacher; you can keep people's attention and teach in a fun way that helped me to learn everything and gave me a solid base for the following years of advanced math. I enjoyed coming to your class every day! – Bradley R., student, 2004-2005

I was not motivated until I went to college later in life and made friends that cared about their education. I was a slug in high school. No teacher motivated me. As for you, I think that your number one trait wasn't so much your ability to teach topics but your extreme love you have for Lackawanna, the school, and your students. Your passion and love of your students is what made you a great teacher. That is your best trait and that made you a great teacher. – Brian F., teacher

Mr. Fiore, you were an amazing teacher who taught me very well the workings of Mathematics, as you were my Algebra teacher in middle school. Your teachings helped me to advance through toward other, more complex math, including Algebra 2 Trig and Calculus. – Bridget W., student, 2010-2012

Mr. Fiore's dedication to students is second to none. Not only does he share his knowledge and love for mathematics with his students, he does it with genuine care. It is rare to find an educator with such skill and enthusiasm combined with genuine compassion for students, yet Mr. Fiore satisfies all three with ease. There is no one I've met more dedicated to the education of young people than him. This fact is obvious to all his students, past or present. His skill, intelligence and diligence helped introduce the world of mathematics to me, a world that I delve deep into each day as an engineering student. I, and I'm sure countless other students, share this sentiment and owe a great amount of our success to him. Mr. Fiore is the prime example of excellence in education: passion for the art of teaching, a love of the subject he teaches and unparalleled dedication to students. – Brittany P., student, 2007-2009

Hi, Mr. Fiore. I got your message on my timeline and some important characteristics of a teacher to me is a teacher who can set high expectations for their students and cares that their students are receiving the best education possible. A teacher who has great communication skills with their students when it comes down to them needing an explanation on a lesson or whatever it may be. A teacher who can provide a welcoming classroom for their students. I feel like if a teacher has all these characteristics a student would have no problem communicating with one because they would look at them as "easy to talk to" and would feel comfortable talking to that teacher about any and everything. – Brittany W., student, 2015-2016

Mr. Fiore is one of the most memorable teachers I have ever had. His devotion and dedication to his craft and students was always was the high point of my learning day. He did more than just reach the curriculum. He made you want to get involved as a student. He saw the hidden potential in people that they may not have seen in themselves and found a way to bring it out of every one of his students, myself included. If there is only one person I can trust to teach myself or family, Mr. Fiore is that man. He was more than just a teacher for me; he was a mentor whether he knows it or not. – Bryan J., student, 2006-2007

I had the privilege of being enrolled in Mr. Fiore's Accelerated Math class for two years in sequence, and this experience has had an immeasurable impact on my education. Mr. Fiore and I had the opportunity to connect and build a relationship over the two years I was in his classes, but due to his personality it only took a few short days before I felt completely comfortable with him. Even as a naïve young adult of middle school age, it is easy to see the passion Mr. Fiore has for teaching and the care he expresses towards his students. – Caleb W., student, 2007-2009

You have always been a role model for me and every student who has ever set foot in your classroom. Your passion for life and every soul you've met is truly remarkable. I only feel bad for the ones who will never have your influence in their lives. You are truly one of a kind. Thank you for inspiring us all. We cannot express your importance enough. – Cameron C., student, 2007-2008

For me one of the most important characteristics about a teacher is, of course, communication and patience. The reason I say this is because a person like me that came from another country to the United States, to have a better education and life, it is important that my teachers communicate with me in a way that I could understand better. With that comes patience because one of my biggest problems was that I couldn't completely understand what they were teaching so I would have more than 3 questions for a simple problem. Sometimes the teacher didn't have the patience to sit down and explain to me word by word. – Carlos S., student, 2015-2016

I've put a lot of thought into what makes a great teacher. I never actually had you as a teacher and I feel that if I did, I may have been more successful in passing math. I'm a fan of the No Child Left Behind era. Unfortunately, I had it rough and nobody cared enough to find out what was going on and I was labeled a troublemaker...rightfully so, because plain and simple math was not my strong point and my teacher sucked. Refused to help me despite knowing I just didn't "get it" so I would do anything just to get out of class. To this day I don't know how to do much more than the basic math it takes to make my world go 'round. I'm great with money and proud to say that for the not so proud recipient of a GED, I have an amazing job and make more than enough for my kids to have a good life... sorry that was a tangent. Anyways, I was envious of your students and very much needed someone who would take their time and get me back on track. That sir is what makes you one of the greatest teachers of all time. You have a passion for teaching and seeing the "aha" come across someone's face as it lights up with the knowledge you instilled in them. – Carolin D., student

I always struggled in math. It was my least favorite subject, and the one I never succeeded at. Until I entered Mr. Fiore's math class in 7th grade, where math became one of my favorite subjects. Math never really clicked with me until this amazing teacher. I have never understood math as strongly as I did than when I was in his class. I never got good grades in math, but in his class, I had high 80's, 90's and even 100's. I've never had such an amazing teacher. He did everything he could for his students and more, his class felt like a family and I was a successful part of it. He took extreme pride in all his students and did everything he could to make sure they understood the material instead of just moving on even if everyone didn't get it. I couldn't have asked for a better teacher. – Casey Jo, student, 2007-2008

You were the only math teacher I've had that's taken the time to make sure I passed & you've been one of my favorite teachers since 7th grade. – Catherine H., student, 2013-2014

I asked Nicole (daughter) what she came away with during her time with you as your student. She said you never gave up on anyone. If someone didn't understand a math problem, you'd explain it as many times as was necessary. As a teacher you never made anyone feel 'dumb' and that anyone could learn any math problem albeit via different steps or explanations. You made the students believe in themselves. – Cherylann M., parent

When discussing teaching pedagogy or methods of instruction, Mr. Fiore and I both agree to keep it simple and realistic, empower confidence, celebrate any and all successes, then build off them. As a genuine believer in our students, their opinion matters to me. Once my students leave me and I see them later, one of my first questions is "Who is your favorite teacher?". Often, the answer is Mr. Fiore. Now why is that prudent? Well, because one would expect the answer to be one of the special area teachers or a teacher of a course that the student has a personal connection to. The students I have posed these questions to are at-risk students who often have given up on academics, for one reason or another. Now therefore it is so impressive, because they choose a teacher of one of the hardest academic areas to learn. Not only does he get through to these students, he takes a personal investment in them. Mr. Fiore not only tries his best to make himself accessible for students while under his instruction, he often helps his students who are having trouble in another math course. – Claire S., teacher

During my time in the Lackawanna City School District, I have had very few teachers like Mr. Peter Fiore. Aside from his outstanding knowledge and mastery

of his profession, he is also a very welcoming and kind person. Mr. Fiore had a way of interacting with students that just made you want to be in his class. Throw a great sense of humor on top of all that and you have one of the most unforgettable teachers I've ever had the honor of learning from. – Cody M., student, 2005-2006

I think the most important thing for a teacher is to find that balance between being personable but also motivating his/her students to learn. I had teachers that were too personable to the point where we didn't really learn anything because we were too busy trying to be friends. I also had teachers that stuck so strictly to the curriculum that I didn't retain anything because the class became tedious and boring. Your class was one of the exceptions to this. You carved out time mostly every day to talk to us about what we liked and were interested in, even if it was something you weren't interested in yourself. Doing that helped us like and respect you, which helped us care about what you were teaching us. You gave us a chance to talk about our interests while still making sure we got our education. I don't think this comes as a surprise, but I was, and to a point still am, rather introverted in nature, so having that few minutes every day where we could talk about the Bills or the Sabres really helped me break out of that shell. There were many other factors that affected my school experience, but for the most part, having a few teachers to talk to really made things easier, and having those teachers be so kind and interested in what I had to say means a lot, and resulted in me being more receptive to what they were teaching me.

I do have an experience to help explain my opinion. I have a passion for animation. I am very interested in graphic design, specifically computer editing, like Photoshop or Premiere. I took 2 years of art, a typing class, and a web page design class to pursue this. I'm sorry to say that my experience in this regard was mostly negative. Maybe it was just unfortunate timing, but the teacher that was supposed to teach typing/web design had a serious medical issue that made him unavailable for the entire year. That's totally understandable, I wasn't upset about it at all. The problem though is that instead of getting a teacher that could teach us what we were there to learn, we had a fan favorite substitute teacher that would spend the class telling us to do whatever we wanted on the computer while talking to us about general stuff. We did maybe 3 typing assignments the whole year, and we didn't learn a single thing about web design. At the time my feeling was "I get a whole class where I get to do basically nothing, this is great!", but now I wish I had gotten to learn more because it would have been very beneficial to me. The only saving grace was my second year of art class. I had Ms. Carducci as my teacher, and I loved her. She was so upbeat and friendly and fun that she made me really want to do well in her class. I would even go after class to paint 2 ceiling tiles, one of which I still have to this day. Had I not had her as my art teacher, my interest in art/animation/web design would probably not exist anymore. – Connor L., student, 2005-2007

I've had the pleasure of knowing Mr. Peter Fiore for many years now and worked side-by-side with him as a colleague at a local public high school. I'm proud to say that he is one of the most dedicated, authentic, motivated, and knowledgeable teachers I've ever seen. I highly recommend Mr. Fiore as an exemplary instructor. He has a proven track record of success. – Craig K., teacher

The most important was the way you portrayed yourself to the students. You always made us feel at home in your classroom and there was never a student that I knew that didn't like you. It's because you always knew what to say and what to do, and when we had problems, we would go to you. – Cristion A., student, 2014-2016

Mr. Fiore was my middle school advanced math teacher for algebra. Mr. Fiore build his students a strong mathematical foundation inside and outside of the classroom. No matter where you were, you could always ask Mr. Fiore for help on any matter such as life. His passion and skill for teaching has been shown in many of his former students have gone on to top Ivy League schools for engineering and/or ended up at a Fortune 500 company. Thank you, Mr. Fiore, for your passion for teaching and I wish you the very best. – Daniel L., 2007-2009

First off, I wanted to say how grateful and appreciative I am to have a teacher like Mr. Fiore. From walking into class on the first day of 7th grade to walking out onto the court or football field Mr. Fiore has always been there to support and hope for the best for me. In the classroom he has, numerous times, help that "light bulb" or that "spark", go off. I always felt welcome to come and ask for help or to even get something off my chest and I am forever grateful for that. Fortunately, I was lucky enough to say I had Mr. Fiore for a teacher and even if you didn't you should without question get to know the man. – Danny E., student, 2012-2013

Having spent 37 years in a secondary English classroom, I had the pleasure of working with many distinguished teachers. Next door to me my third year of teaching was Peter Fiore. Peter was able to make the most complex mathematical concepts understandable for ALL students. His knowledge, dedication, passion and genuine concern for his students was inspiring.

Peter, I remember someone once telling me that if you are going to cover material without giving it meaning, you might as well cover it with dirt because it is dead anyway. That, my friend, from what I have read from your former students' testimonials and from what I recollect teaching next door to you years ago, was the essence of your teaching. You taught young people math; you did not teach math to young people. Putting the student first made all the difference! – David C., teacher

You know I always appreciate it. Man, thanks for being a very influential teacher to me. You've taught me a lot and I can never thank you enough for it. – David H., student, 2008-2010

Have you ever listened to music and wished that you could sing just like the artist that you were listening to? People tend to wish that they could be just like the professionals that do the things they want to do. I was never really into music, but I sure do have a similar experience.

I was always intrigued by mathematics as a young student. I began thinking about what I wanted to do with the rest of my life, but I could never decide. This was until I began my life changing year in Mr. Fiore's algebra class. His teaching ability, to this day, is still unmatched by any other teacher that I have seen in a classroom (and I have been in classrooms for over 17 years now). Mr. Fiore was able to scaffold his lessons in such a way that the top students were always attentive and challenged, while the lower level students in the classroom were able to confidently say that they understood the material. Mr. Fiore always assessed the knowledge of the students with exit slips or journal entries that kept him informed on what the students understood and what he needed to spend a little more time on.

At the end of the year, those of us who produced the grades we strived for were cemented into the "Wall of Fame" that lined the perimeter of the classroom. The Wall of Fame was a collection of all the students who received grades of mastery on either their overall averages for all quarters and/or a mastery level grade on the Regents examination. This was the ultimate form of motivation that made all of Mr. Fiore's students strive to do their best. I saw the command that Mr. Fiore had over the class firsthand. He was the perfect combination of strict and friendly which made me want to succeed not only for myself, but to make him proud as well. To this day I remember all that Mr. Fiore did in his classes and I one day aspire to be just as good as him. Since this class, I started concentrating on a career to become a Math teacher just like the man that I wished I could be just like. Mr. Fiore is not just an educator; he is an idol of mine and a role model as well. – David R., student, 2006-2008

You are such an amazing teacher! You have a style of teaching and explaining concepts that makes anyone understand them, no matter how complex, and you are always there for help. Not only that, but you are so involved in the school and such a respected figure. In our school, you were such a positive influence, be it in our education or our lives in general :) You truly are an amazing teacher. I wish that there were more teachers like you. – Delaney S., student, 2013-2014

Looking back on middle/high school from what I can remember, all my teachers weren't just there to collect a paycheck. They all truly cared about every student's education and helping them succeed. They all pushed students to go beyond just passing and celebrated our success with us. My teachers had an unfathomable amount of patience whether it was dealing with unruly stubborn students to the ones who needed a little extra help to grasp the lessons being taught. Being graduated for 11 years now makes me appreciate all the effort my teachers put in even though they rarely get a thank you from students themselves. The workloads we would get as students was more than fair. Enough to challenge us and help us learn but not so much to take up all our free time. Especially in the later years of high school when courses got tougher, and extracurriculars became more frequent and time consuming. My experiences in your class, Mr. Fiore, were nothing but pleasurable. Being in the advance math classes was a little intimidating at the time, but with the passion you had toward the subject made it that much easier. You taught in ways that made it easier for us to understand. You took pride in us when we achieved and worked harder if we were struggling. You also gave us breaks and lightened the class when we were approaching holiday breaks. That to me is a great quality in a teacher. – Derrick M., student, 2002-2004

Greatest math teacher. You would break the problem down and make sure we understood it. You would emphasis the steps it took to do every math problem the right way. – Diamond S., student, 2008-2010

Relateability (made up word) is one of the most important attributes a teacher can have. Being able to relate to one's students, to build rapport, then use that rapport to create a model which can be understood, is critical to learning. Rapport which is genuine is critical. If a teacher really cares about the student, and their outcome, it is tough to hide. That care comes out. Mass Maritime taught me the theory of learn, do, learn. The practical application of this kept me engaged, kept me focused. Captains who genuinely cared about their students kept the audience. Rowdy young men stayed engaged when an old Captain explained what would keep them alive. My own experience becoming a teacher as a Captain has been humbling. Being humble is a wonderful tool in teaching. Humility can be felt, and it supports genuine instruction. – Drew M., parent

In my time at Lackawanna Middle and High School one thing was always clear to me even before I became your student in the 2009-10 school year: you were teaching for way more than just a paycheck. You were teaching for the love of the kids and to try and make future generations as successful as possible, in and out of the classroom. You were more than a teacher you made time for every student and where there for them rather it was for math or any other subject, advice, life problems, sports or just needed someone to talk to. In the classroom you altered you lessons so every student could understand what was being taught unlike many teachers. Out of the classroom you attended and helped with as many sporting events as possible, wrote heart felt college and employment recommendation letters and did all you possibly could to see myself and many other take that next step in life in a way we would be successful. Now as your teaching days at Lackawanna have come to an end you are still around all the time still helping the students and alumni be successful, you are still at every possible sporting event you can be at, and I know to this day and in the future I can come to you at any time without judgement. Thank you for being the greatest Teacher, Mentor, and Friend all the Steelers Family could as for. – Dyllen O., student, 2009-2010

Some of the more important characteristics of being a teacher to me in high school was a positive upbeat vibe, telling stories (which you had some great ones), and fun ways to have the material taught. Being in all advanced classes my school career I will have different views than others because I take my education serious. With that, from a student standpoint I feel education is a gateway to success and it critical to have a good grasp on how to make your education worth it. Having you as a teacher in class you encompassed everything that made education worthwhile. – Edward B., student, 2012-2013

7th grade, one of the toughest years in middle school. As a student, I've always struggled in math; however, I had the pleasure of having one of the greatest math teachers I know. Thanks to you I learned a lot of important lessons, not just in math. You never treated your students poorly, never made someone feel like less

101

of a student and always had open arms to anyone who needed remediation. I will never forget the teacher you are, and you made a great impact on me as a student. Good luck with retirement, God knows you've earned it! – Elise O., student, 2013-2014

I had the pleasure of having Mr. Fiore as a math teacher in 8th grade. He is a teacher who goes above and beyond for his students. He is an outstanding teacher whose enthusiasm, dedication and approach to inspire students to thrive to succeed. He always made sure that his students were prepared and confident in what they were doing. I am happy I had the opportunity to be his student. He will continue doing great things. I wish you nothing but the best, Mr. Fiore. – Elizabeth S., student, 2003-2004

Growing up I never could relate, I never felt good enough, but Mr. Fiore's class was the one thing I remember that started my evolution into an adult. His ability to relate to his students through their interests, open communication and never belittling anyone are the biggest lessons he's taught me. He would treat you like an adult and always would give you a shot. He expected us to perform in his classroom and behave outside of it. I've had some good teachers, but no one comes close, and it's easy to tell the difference, as no one cares more about their students. Children need to be supported and influenced and Mr. Fiore is a great role model for all teachers. All this from a math class, best teacher ever! – Emir M., student, 2003-2005

Excellent instructor whose pedagogical techniques I employ well over a decade later. Very parent-like in the way he cares for his students and wants us all to succeed. – Fayzah A., student, 2002-2004

Personally, the best teachers I've ever had always put their heart into what they did and choose to get to know the students on a personal level. When the students were having trouble teachers would have the knowledge and trust with the student to assess where they were going wrong and to help fix the problems. When a teacher is simply in the school environment for a paycheck it isn't benefiting anyone besides themselves. – Felicia A., student, 2012-2014

One universal thing that I noticed that I liked was having a teacher that was tough on the students but cared for the student and was primarily tough knowing that the student could excel in that subject. For example, last semester, I had a rocky start to Business Calc and struggled for the first little bit and the teacher was tough about it. This caused for an awakening for me to get my act together and put more time in. Another thing is how you used to put the NYS CC exam test scores on a poster. That was a good confidence booster and it was able to push students to do better trying to get at the top of the list. – Gary A., student, 2012-2013

Mr. Fiore was the BEST teacher I ever had. He cared more about seeing his students succeed than anything. He would answer any question you had in any amount of detail he could muster until you understood what you needed to. Not only is he a great teacher, but he is a great person. He has so much compassion for teaching and his students. Going back to his class for a visit after my first semester of high school showed me how nothing has changed. No matter where Mr. Fiore ends up, he will make it a better place, and a place where students will love to learn and love being there, from his company alone! Thank you so much for being my teacher for middle school and being my drive to be the person I am today! – Gene O., student, 2009-2011

One of the best teachers I ever had was a History Professor at the University of Rochester- I still see his name in the news at times. He was already prominent in his field, but I can remember being in his class, and not taking notes- not ever. He spoke of history as a story- like no other, and he knew his stuff, and loved it. And because he did, he was able to make it come alive for all of us. – Ginny Z., friend

You were the best teacher!!! No matter how much I wanted to give up & said I can't you pushed me & told me I could! Until this day I believe if it was not for you & Mr. O I would have never passed math & graduated. For that I will forever be grateful!!! – Hailey Z., student, 2015-2016

Personally, I find it easier to learn when teachers have a good sense of humor and always have good energy in the classroom. When the teacher keeps the learning environment light and humorous it helps us as students relax more, which then leads to us learning the content with more ease. – Haley D., student, 2012-2013

One of the most important characteristics of a teacher, in my opinion, is patience. I think it's so much easier for a student to learn if the instructor doesn't put a time frame on it. I understand that there's a certain curriculum with limited time, but I just mean, understanding that not everyone learns at the same rate or in the same ways. Which is another important characteristic—versatility. From what I remember from seventh grade which seems like a lifetime ago, you were a very versatile teacher. I hated math and wasn't very good at it but the way you taught made sense to me and I understood things I hadn't before. Like our math notebooks with the indexes, that was cool. Some of my most favorite teachers were funny, kind, open minded, and listened to their students' ideas instead of just lecturing and lecturing. The patience thing is something I must practice, as I want to be an English teacher and I have none. – Hannah F., student, 2012-2013

His classroom was always a welcoming place. Mr. Fiore was—without a doubt— one of the most encouraging and supportive teachers I had as a child. He pushed his students to excel in and out of the classroom, coming to many of the school's sporting events and cheering us on and getting involved in the school musical with a cameo every year. He pushed middle schoolers into intellectual thought, disguising them as discussion questions during homeroom or a break in a block-period class. There is simply no better teacher to tutor a child in mathematics. Mr. Fiore's passion for teaching and helping his students shine is nearly unparalleled. I've been blessed with a bounty of fabulous teachers throughout my years in school, but Mr. Fiore sticks out among the best of the best. – Hannah G., student, 2007-2009

It is with great pleasure that I write this letter of support for Mr. Peter Fiore. I have had the honor of being taught by Mr. Fiore before his retirement from Lackawanna High School. Not only is he a wonderful teacher, but a lovely person as well. Mr. Fiore adapts his teaching skills to each student and their specific academic needs. Mr. Fiore has always set high, but not unreasonable, standards for his students while supplying tools and skills required to succeed.

You were one of the teachers in my lifetime this far that stood out. You cared the extra bit in every situation, you were a friend, you were our family. I still have every Beatles album you made me a copy of. I take every opportunity to tell people about how much that extra mile as a teacher can impact a student. I'll say this until my dying breath: you are one of the greatest educators in the world. – Hannah S., student, 2011-2012

Many inexperienced, or untalented history teachers, concentrate on the "who and when" - names and dates. They miss the very important "how, what and why". A good history teacher will remove a variable and inquire, "how would today's world be different"? Majoring in history, I had many professors like that. I owe them more than I could ever possibly repay. They taught me to think critically, question things & never accept anything at face value - dig, dig, dig - sometimes the truth is buried deep. A career in Quality Assurance broadened this - corrective action, finding the root cause, etc. – Harry G., friend

Your teaching abilities are no match for many. You are always determined to help a student in need. Even if you had to stay after on your own time to make sure to help a student succeed. – Haylee N., student, 2015-2016

Mr. Fiore was one of the most helpful and amazing teachers I've ever had. He was extremely friendly and never got frustrated with you no matter how long it took

him to explain something to you. Math was one of my most difficult subjects in school and he made it easy and extremely fun for me to learn something. He always stayed with you for if you needed him to and was always willing to help no matter what. I will always appreciate everything he has done for me throughout my years when I was in school, and really making it easier for me to understand math better than I ever could have thought. – Heather C., student, 2009-2010

I used to tell my grade level colleagues all the funny things my kindergarteners said every day. One of the teachers said she didn't know why my class was so funny and hers is not. I didn't have the heart to tell her that I listened to my kids. They say things all the time, but you need to listen to hear them.

When I was teaching just a couple of years ago, I used a Smartboard. It was very handy. If we were discussing whales, I could find YouTube videos about them instantly. Of course, I also read books about them, but it was great to show the difference between a toothed whale and a baleen whale as we talked about them. If we were dancing, I could find an old song I loved instantly. Of course, we had time to talk and I listened to all my kindergarteners, too. I would not use the technology all the time, but it was handy. One time I was at a restaurant in town and as my husband and I talked about our family, I noticed a large family sitting at a round table near us. There were 10 of them of all ages. Not one was talking or looking at each other the whole time. They were looking down at their phones. I was so sad! They had the perfect opportunity to share and laugh and connect, but they did not. We must have limits and not be addicted to this technology. When my grandchildren come over, we do things together. We have the time to listen and talk and ask questions without rushing. Occasionally they will ask to see something on the computer, and we say no. Then we move on to doing something. My grandson wanted me to teach him to knit just a couple of days ago. My granddaughter wanted Grandpa to chase her around the house. It was ok without a phone or computer! – Helen W., teacher

In my freshman year of high school, my pre-algebra math teacher was Mr. Fiore. Usually, I struggle with math. I never received the extra help I needed from past teachers. But Mr. Fiore made sure everyone was familiar with the subject he was teaching. Regardless if it was going over the subject on the overhead or going to every one of us until he knew we were all familiar. My 9th grade year of math was my best, passing his class in the high 90's. Also, it was hard to fall asleep in his class. Mr. Fiore always kept his class interesting. He had spirit for his school & students. – Hunter W., student, 2015-2016

Out of all the Math teachers I've ever had, I have to say Mr. Fiore was the best without a doubt! He explained things very well. Whenever I needed a little more help on understanding the work, he helped me right away and didn't stop explaining things to me until I understood the Math completely. Mr. Fiore never gave up on his students, he kept pushing them until they succeeded. For example, when I struggled to pass the Algebra Regents exam it took many attempts to pass it and right as my breaking point was about to occur, Mr. Fiore came along and stayed by my side till I knew enough material to get me to pass the exam. When I went in for the third time for the Algebra exam, I was very confident, and eventually I got a call from Mr. Fiore saying I finally passed with a score of 70! I wouldn't have been able to do it without such an amazing, supportive teacher. Thanks again, Mr. Fiore, you're the best! – Iceis C., student, 2012-2013, 2015-2016

Mr. Fiore taught two out of three of my daughters. They loved him as their teacher. According to my girls, they looked forward to his class because Mr. Fiore made learning math fun, he kept it interesting, and whenever they needed the extra help, he was always willing to take the extra time needed. – Irma F., parent

You have a knack for making people realize their full potential. Without you as a math teacher, I would have never believed I was smart enough. You never made me feel like a mistake was the end of the world. Instead, you told me how to fix it and said everyone makes mistakes. I really must thank you for being one of the best teachers I've ever had. – Jamielynne F., student, 2006-2008

Growing up, I've had a lot of trouble with my education due to myself having to learn two languages and my parents not fully grasping the English language, so trying to help me with my schoolwork was a challenge. It took me a while to become fully motivated in bettering my education, until I reached middle school and met an amazing math teacher. Mr. Fiore, you have made a huge impact in my life and to many others. Some of the high qualities that you have that made you a great teacher was having a deep knowledge and passion for educating students, a strong work ethic, developing care in building relationships with the students, and most importantly, believing in each and every one of us to be the best that we can be! You were open to help anyone who were having trouble with their grades and many always looked up to you because of this. All of this really encouraged and pushed me to better myself and be the best that I could be! This also motivated me to help others to be the best that they could be as well. For instantly, this past year I was in the LPN nursing school and many of the students were having trouble with math. You had to receive an 85% or above in order to pass, and if you failed that with one more other class, you were dropped. Many were struggling with a below average, so I offered them my own time to tutor them if need be and a lot of them took that offer. They were able to walk the stage and receive their diploma. To this day, I will always know that if it wasn't for me, many of them would have been dropped all because of the math course and many of them still tell me that to this day. Whenever I hear that, all I say in my head is, "Thanks to Mr. Fiore!" So, I thank you for giving me hope and high expectations, as I was able to pass this along to others. – Jasmina O., student, 2007-2009

Mr. Fiore is the best math teacher I ever had. He explains the material in a way that no other teacher did. He made sure everyone knew the material before he moved on so no one would get lost. My highest average was in his class thanks to the way he taught Mathematics. Not to mention he helped get me into St. Francis with a little scholarship because of my grades (math). Mr. Fiore would be the first to get to school and the last to leave if someone needed help. Thank you, Mr. Fiore, for having the best class ever. – Jayden D., student, 2014-2015

Dedication. I will never forget the time that you spent with me in 8 grade math. I am not sure you remember but you would pick me up every morning at 5:30am and tutor me before classes. That's what I remember. Dedication!!! – Jennifer H., student, 1978-1979

Math seems to be one of those subjects where you either understand or you don't with very little in between. Your teaching capabilities changed that. You always made sure that everything was thoroughly explained and brought a liveliness to learning algebra. Questions were never left unanswered and math became one of my best subjects. You have always gone out of your way to help whether it was math skills or life advice. Success was always a tangible concept under your lessons...I speak only the truth. You sparked a passion for math in me that I honestly believe allowed me to become interested in engineering. Great teaching equals great success and without doubt you are beyond great. No one could ignite a spark of learning, determination, acceptance, and compassion quite like you, Mr. Fiore. Good teachers teach. Great teachers inspire their students to become their very best selves. We all love you.

Educators are far more important to our society than I believe we give credit to. Many of us are going to receive nearly two decades of formal education. That's nearly a fourth of our lives. Good educators understand this. They take this time to inspire and fuel a prosperous future far longer than their own lives and legacy. Being an educator takes selflessness, dedication, and above all, a passion in knowing that even igniting just one mind to pursue a hunger for knowledge is a job well done. As we stand currently, I believe the American education system is not nurturing our young citizens' minds in a way that creates happy, healthy adults. Therefore, our educators are so valuable. Great educators break the rigid mold of standardized testing and transform learning from scores and statistics into a yearning to become your best self in hopes to make a positive impact in our world. It takes a special kind of heart and soul to be an educator; making them, perhaps, one our most valuable resources. – Jennifer M., student, 2011-2012

I have the privilege of writing about one of the finest educators I've known. I was an 8th grade student of Mr. Fiore at Lackawanna Middle School. He was my math teacher that year, and at that age, math class was just a nuisance. I couldn't think of any situation in which the Pythagorean Theorem would be necessary knowledge to have in life. Consequently, up until that year, I usually gave math class about 50% of my attention. Mr. Fiore's class was different. He managed his class with discipline, and it was well understood by all of us that his class was not the class you wanted to be in trouble in. He was never willing to let someone fall behind and was always able to present material in a way that made it easy to understand. It's been 17 years that I sat in his class, and I can speak with tremendous confidence in Mr. Fiore's ability as an educator. I know I am just one of many former students who can now look back and appreciate the value of having had him as a teacher. – Jeremy C., student, 2001-2002

I just remember coming into 8th grade at Lackawanna Middle School... I never was good at math never believed in myself enough to get by. I always talked down on myself because I never understood. But when I came into your class you really inspired me, Mr. Fiore. I just remember you saying "See, Jerid, I was sure you can do it"! After having you as a teacher I always believed in myself. Good luck, Mr. Fiore. – Jerid V., student, 2014-2015

Peter Fiore was an impeccable teacher. He made learning fun for me and got me some of the highest grades I've had in over 2 years. He made Common Core math easier for me to understand and is just, all in all, a fantastic teacher. I can remember back to eighth grade that you were my math teacher and you just got everyone to connect with you. Your math class was the first math class I enjoyed and had high grades in because you were able to make it realistic. You could turn a problem into a real-life scenario that we'd all be able to understand. And even after your retirement from Lackawanna you helped me pass my algebra exam which I'd failed the year before. You made everything in math seem so simplified to what it really looked like. – Jerred L., student, 2014-2015

Mr. Fiore, I believe you are an inspiring individual. You are a role model that any person should strive to become. I believe you are the pinnacle of what any educator should hope to achieve. Your passion for teaching others cannot be questioned. You motivated and set high expectations for your students giving anyone of them their chance to succeed. While I was not one of these students, the wisdom you have instilled upon me has helped shape me into the person I am today. You should be nothing less than proud. – Jesse K., student

I was honored to be in Mr. Fiore's first advanced math class. Where almost 30 students were chosen to be under Mr. Fiore's wing when we all tested above the average Math level. If it wasn't for Mr. Fiore, we would not have had the confidence to keep going on our adventure of being ahead of our graduating class in the Math world. Mr. Fiore opened the door for us and showed all 30 of us what potential we had and how much we all loved a challenge. I am lucky that I had him to open that door for me many years ago. I went on to test out of 2 other classes as well (science and history) because of the confidence I had from Mr. Fiore. If it was not for the drive to excel that he gave his students, I would not have graduated high school with 9 college credits! He never gave up on us, he kept pushing us to be better, not only at math but as human beings. His passion for math, teaching and leading others to be great is an amazing quality to have. Thank you, Mr. Fiore, for being you and opening the door to opportunity for us all. – Jessica T., student, 2001-2002

One day in 1978 or so, you were just being a cool Math teacher shooting the shit with a bunch of seventh graders (which was awesome) and the subject of favorite bands came up. You mentioned being really into Aerosmith and "Toys in the Attic" in particular. I figured if cool dude Mr. Fiore was into them, they had to good. That set me on a path to loving all the great classic rock that I still love and listen to as well as play. It was life changing to see a teacher as a regular person and shared a glimpse of their out-of-school life with us kids....and you were a damn good Math teacher too! I can still vividly recall that day in Hoover Jr. High...Thanks for more than just Math lessons. – Joe D., student, 1977-1978

You approach every day and every student with passion. You held your standards high and made us reach them unlike many teachers who lowered the standards to meet the class. One lesson in life I learned from you is there is always a solution to every problem. If you learn the basic principles, have patience and determination, all problems are solved! You and Mr. Porter will forever be my guiding beacons. – Joe D., student, 1978-1979

I had the privilege of working with Peter Fiore for over 15 years. Over those years I have personally seen his talents as a master Math teacher in the classroom as well as outside the classroom. Peter is the type of teacher that does not just punch in and punch out each day. I have witnessed many times where he has taken his time (before, during and after school) to help students to achieve their very best. Peter believes in his students! By saying this, I mean he knows that every student can learn and be successful in Math as well as any other class. He has spent countless years perfecting his craft. I believe that there is no better teacher out there who could do as good a job as Peter Fiore can! – Joe T., teacher

I was a student of Mr. Fiore's back in middle school some 40 years ago. While in his class he treated all students with dignity and respect. His methods of teaching were above any other teacher I had, and he conveyed the information effectively. Thus, I was able to score a 95 for my final grade in math. My son back in 2014 failed math. The following year, with Mr. Fiore as his teacher, he got a 92 average. For this, I feel it's the teacher that makes the student. I feel Mr. Fiore's teaching skills exceed those of his counterparts. His relationships with his students go on unscathed due to his professionalism, caring, and ability to keep a student's attention by good communication skills. – John G., student, 1978-1979

If you only had time to do one homework assignment, you chose to do your math for Mr. Fiore. Not because of fear or intimidation but because you wanted to get to the next lesson. The energy level of that class made the work exciting! Not an

easy task for quadratic equations! Mr. Fiore made the lessons fun and that made the learning easier! That's great teaching!

Coaching cliché stolen from Jim Calhoun- U Conn: "Kids don't care how much you know until they know how much you care!" Some teachers show how little they care far too often! It becomes obvious they are there to get paid, not to teach! – John O., student, 1979-1980

Good teachers to me are the ones that are always willing to work one on one with a student when they don't understand things even when they have a lesson plan. – Joseph K., student, 2013-2014

Throughout school after say, 4th grade, you really begin to feel the weight of your classes and need to take things more seriously. From having a solid morning routine to having a positive attitude during classes, it really goes a long way. When it comes to your teachers, they can almost be seen like your friends in a way. You come into their room every day and they show off all their cool stuff, as if you walked into a friend's house and he showed you all his cool souvenirs or pictures from a vacation. You come in and like most people, you don't want to be there. We all get it; we've all been there; this doesn't mean that the teachers don't want to be there either. One of the most important aspects of a teacher is how they portray themselves in class, their energy and attitude in class show how much they want to be there, and how much they WANT to teach you, rather than slaving away with kids during the day, to go home and work on papers or prepare materials for future classes. Students come in and well, on most cases this persona about the teacher affects how the students act, how attentive they are and overall affects the class. A teacher must be strict enough to be able to remove or punish students that are overly out of hand, but also be able to work with the students personally. Figure out problems on situations, give the individual attention they need. Being able to be flexible with schedules, classroom procedures and being open to new ideas even from the students themselves is also very important. Being able to keep a good mindset in the classroom, work attentively and yet be able to sell to the students what you're trying to teach them and making sure that each one of them gets the proper attention they need to understand the material. It's the teacher's job to get through to those he is teaching and when they finally pass, the teacher can know he or she did a good job in the classroom. These are all important and really what I look for in a teacher when I enter their classroom every day for a school year. – Joshua K., student

I think the first thing a teacher should be is understanding, understand that every student is different and has different learning curves. They should always try to make a connection with a student and realize that if a student doesn't follow rules and disrupts classrooms that maybe the student has something going on at home and just need someone to talk to. Finally, I believe there are some teachers that try too hard instead of just being themselves, a student would have a lot more respect for a teacher that they feel isn't just a teacher but an actual person just like them that is looking out for his/her students. – Justin D., student, 2012-2013

I had the great pleasure of being in Mr. Fiore's first math class he ever taught. Not only was (is) he a great teacher, he was a major contributor to my love for Math. He always showed a passion for Math and teaching in general and continued to mentor me throughout my high school years. He shows great knowledge and wisdom and his teachings have become great life lessons for me. He truly leaves an impact on every student he encounters, and I couldn't have hand picked a better person to have as a teacher. – Kathleen W., student, 2001-2002

Best teacher ever, strict enough to get things in our heads and make things light enough to completely understand. You're willing to help any student and push them to the max. No other teacher like you! – Kayla O., student, 2013-2014

I had the pleasure of having Mr. Fiore as my teacher for both 7th and 8th grade Advanced Math. He is one of the greatest individuals that I had known. Not only is he a spectacular teacher, he continuously went above and beyond to make sure that all his students felt prepared and confident not only about the Math that was being done in class but for the duration of the school day. If there was one thing that he made apparent in class everyday was to try your best and never doubt yourself in anything that you did. This man taught me so much and I cannot thank him enough! I know you are going to continue to do great things and I wish you nothing but the best, Mr. Fiore! – Kenneth S., student, 2007-2009

You & Mr. Korach were the last of a dying breed. You focused not only on doing the coursework timely and accurately, but with integrity as well. Congrats on your retirement. Your good fortune is a loss for both the teaching community and for those students that won't get to have you as their teacher. I still tell everyone that bothers to ask that were the best teacher I ever had. You made a difference. – Kevin R., student, 1979-1980

You were one of the most motivating teachers I ever had, you are unmatched in the classroom with your passion and dedication. – Kevin S., student, 2005-2007

It's been a long time since Mr. Fiore taught me advanced math, but I can never forget how, because of him, I came to love Math! I never cared for it as much until I had him for a teacher. I was okay at Math, but the passion and enthusiasm he has while teaching was contagious! And it's those very qualities that make an impression in everyday life. His approach at making his teaching environment a great learning experience for all his students was exceptional. He always pushed us beyond our limits because of the belief he had in us, and it was always a good time in his classes! It takes a great teacher who truly cared about our success to turn us into great students. And he never forgot to acknowledge us in our own skill set which was very important to a young mind! His love for Math always showed and it wasn't just about the classroom setting. It's real-world with the approach he has. I will be forever grateful that I had him as a teacher so long ago. And we were lucky to have him! – Khadeeja S., student, 2001-2002

I still remember the day I was told I was selected to Mr. Fiore's eight-grade advanced math class. It was a pivotal point in my life that influenced me greatly. The subject material was quite challenging to me at the time, but with Mr. Fiore's guidance and with the way that he can connect to his students only the way Mr. Fiore can, I was able to succeed in my studies. Looking back, I am grateful and honored to have been a member of Mr. Fiore's math class. I learned that with hard work and dedication the possibilities are endless. Although I am not currently pursuing a career in mathematics, I will always carry with me the lessons learned as a wide-eyed eighth grader in Mr. Fiore's math class. – Khaled A., student, 2002-2003

As a new student to Lackawanna in 8th grade, with terrible math skills, being in Mr. Fiore's class always helped me feel confident, not only with my math skills but in myself in general. It was always a fun class and I knew that if I needed help with anything that he would be right there. Not only a great teacher but an amazing man. – Kimberly W., student, 2008-2009

I think it says a lot about a teacher when almost 17 years after having been taught by them you hold them on the same pedestal as you did back then. Mr. Fiore's no-nonsense approach set aside any distractions and got down to work. He explained math in a way that made sense and didn't stop until every student had their "aha!" moment. To say teaching was "just a job" to him would be insulting. He served not only as a math teacher but as a role model and an example of how to carry yourself. – Kristen P., student, 2001-2002

I'm glad I was already able to experience having you as a teacher and a mentor... There are people in this world that no matter how long it's been their memory has made an impression on your life and heart. You were a great teacher. – Krystal G., student, 2003-2006

When I think about all the teachers I have had in my life, the ones that have made the greatest impact on me and the ones that continue to impact and influence my life are the ones that strived to connect with me (and other students). It could be something as simple as enjoying the same book, but when a teacher showed that they had a general interest in something I cared about, it showed me that they cared about more than just receiving a paycheck. – Kyle S., student, 2001-2002

You are still to this day one of the best teachers I have ever had. You always believed in us and pushed us to be our best and in turn made us believe in ourselves. You made a difficult subject seem easy to me. This caring and passionate demeanor is what I believe to be most important in teachers. You also had a sense of humor that brought the subject to life and made learning fun.

Unfortunately, many students do not come from the best homes or have families to push them, help them, and lift their self-esteem. I think that it is so important for teachers to help do that for their students. – Lauren K., student, 2006-2008

Mr. Fiore, I'd be more than willing to give you aspects on what I believe makes the best teacher. I'm not saying this because you asked me but you're the best teacher I've ever had. Four years has gone by and I have yet to find a teacher like you. You made what most kids would hate fun. You brought the real world into your teachings just make it so different. I believe a teacher should inspire their students every day. Push them every day to their best. When kids are excited to go to your class, you're doing something right. Taking time to help students to the best of your abilities. Bringing in real life situations to draw in their attention. Not only teaching but you're involved in students' lives. You care about them and what happens with them, you're involved multiple sports. Your encouragement has helped people thrive to be someone better. Being a teacher should help mold a child's future and I believe that's what you did. – Leah B., student, 2014-2015

Of course, the answer to the question is a person who can teach their subject well and thus allow every student to pass, but as I move onto college, I'm starting to realize it's more than that. To be a good teacher, you must care for your students. Show them that you WANT them to pass and make it genuine! Don't just be a nonchalant talking robot! Kids and teenagers need that push; they need to know that you care about them as a person even more than you do as a student in order to propel academically. In my opinion, kindness goes a long way, especially in teaching! Be stern when you must, of course, but don't forget that this is one of the most crucial developing stages of those kids lives. Emotions are running high in their worlds at that time and being aware of their sensitivity is important! Compassion is the answer, always! – Leyla S., student, 2012-2013

Hi Mr. Fiore, I apologize for the late response to your FB post to my wall. I just wanted to say thank you for being the person you are. You always look out for your students to the best of your ability and always willing to help. Math was always far from one of my strongest subjects, but I do appreciate everything you helped me with. I just wish I would have tried harder though, but you live, and you learn. This is just a personal thought/opinion on education or any kind of guidance - but I'd have to agree as the saying goes-"you can lead a horse to water but you can't make him drink" P.S. it's really neat that you're writing a book & hope all is well! – Lindsey L., student, 2003-2004

Peter Fiore has taught my children Math. He inspired them to want to try and try it again until they had a firm grasp on the concepts being taught. They learned the math, without getting frustrated. Mr. Fiore showed patience and understanding for students with learning disabilities, and for students who were easily frustrated with the math curriculum. He displayed a passion for the subject matter, and truly enjoyed working with the students. He easily related to them, and they to him. He has formed bonds of respect with former students that are maintained to this day. – Lisa D., parent

Mr. Fiore, you had sent me a message to give any feedback for your book you are writing. As a parent we always encouraged our children to do their best. We were hands on parents. We both worked but always made our children come first. We both made sure one of us would attend any open house, parent conference as well as any activity they were a part of. We have lived in Lackawanna for over 30 years and sometimes people would comment negatively about our school system. We never gave it another thought about raising our children in this community. Our children went to school from Pre-K to 12th grade. They were surrounded by a diverse population. They had wonderful teachers that helped them develop into the men they are today. You were both Anthony and Andrews advanced math teacher. They both had a gift with math growing up and you were one of the teachers that kept that passion alive. They continued their education throughout high school always taking the advance classes and getting the most out of high school. They both pursued Mechanical Engineering at University at Buffalo and both employed in their field. Anthony works for Center Point Energy in Minneapolis, Minnesota and loves his job. While Andrew is working at Northrup Grumman in Williamsville. Yes, we are very proud of them and that they are independent and have found success. Children can succeed if you give them positive reinforcement and I feel they got it from their family as well as the teachers from Lackawanna schools. – Lisa L., parent

Mr. Fiore is undoubtedly the best Math teacher I've ever had and not only that, he's one of the best teachers I've ever heard of. For the four years that I've known Mr. Fiore he has proven to be very patient with students and really excels at pushing them to reach their designated goals. His door was always open for extra help and never rejected anyone who was willing to put in the work to a better student. In closing, Mr. Fiore is an amazing teacher who was awesome to have. He has not only been a teacher in the classroom but outside of it as well. Over these years I've known him, he's not only looked at as my teacher, but a great friend as well. – London S., student, 2012-2013

A student's grade is a direct reflection of the type of teacher they have. Mr. Fiore made it easy for me to learn a difficult subject, it was the only time I had high 80's/90's in a math class. He was there even when I didn't have him as a teacher.

To me he was one of the best teachers I've ever had! Thank you, Mr. Fiore! – Lydia B., student, 2011-2013

The most essential characteristic of a teacher is respect gained through the teacher being able to tap into the child's "ah ha ... I understand". – Lynn K., student, 1977-1978

Mr. Fiore is more than a teacher. He is a practitioner in his field in fact. I always struggled with math as if a new language (and English was my second language) as an ESL student I struggled with comprehension in many subjects in school, however that all changed when I was assigned Mr. Fiore for math my 8th grade year. I was so thrilled to go class that I enjoyed attending class, because he explained difficult problems with ease, that even I could understand him. It's sad to leave his class, I wished and would have payed to have an instructor like this follow me throughout the years. I support any suggestions this gentleman recommends because it will help.

A good teacher must have good etiquette and manners. This shows students how to treat one another instead of ridicule. A good teacher is knowledgeable in the subject they are teaching. To the degree where they can explain complex concept very simply. A great teacher SMILES a lot to put students at ease, the world isn't going to end. Most importantly the greatest teachers are compassionate. These qualities and attributes have significantly changed many lives whether in class or out. – Mahfoudh S., student, 2004-2005

I have been horrible at math all my life, but in 7th grade you showed me that it didn't matter how bad I was, if I put my mind to it, I could achieve it. Having you as my teacher brought my grade to the upper 90's in math and I could never be so thankful. You are full of cheer, and life and are so caring. Education is so much easier with a teacher who loves the students and loves what they're doing and that's you! I'll never forget you and that year of my life!

For education to flourish it needs teachers who care. When a teacher shows how passionate they are about what they are teaching it can truly resonate with students, it shows them how dedicated the person is to their studies. Throughout my entire education I had certain teachers I knew would push me to do better and those were the teachers I'd look forward to seeing each day. I believe the students who have a strong connection with a teacher are far more likely to attend school.

There is a story that resonates with me about teachers. In the 7th grade I was in your math class. Prior to your class I had always failed math and done horrible. Most of my teachers would give up on me and just give me a passing grade to move on. You were different. You showed passion in your work, you proved to me that you were there for me and my education. You helped me in class, after class, and whenever you had time. I was doing well. It came time for a big test at the end of the year and I was terrified. You gave me words of encouragement and told me not to give up. I took the test - and I got a 90 on it! That was the best grade I have ever received in math (still to this day). At that moment I knew I needed to work on my math skills myself, but I also knew that the teacher had a lot to do with my success in the classroom. Thank you for always being so great. Teachers. They're the golden ticket through education. The BEST teachers show passion, dedication, an understanding that sometimes they're the only hope for students who have no one who cares at home. I'll never forget the teachers I made connections with. I'll carry those moments with me throughout my life because they were important in so many more ways than one. It was never just a math test; it was a life lesson. – Maja M., student, 2009-2010

My opinion. I suppose I just loved the way you presented yourself every day at every giving moment of the day during the hallway and even your experience with your students as well, you made it so much more easier to help me understand the process of learning math you did special techniques using multiple different sports and the best part about it you seemed to be enthusiastic while doing your job which meant you took it very seriously and loved doing it which also helped people remember the problems because. They loved the way you talked about things. Another thing I loved the way you awarded good behavior and good grades. – Malik S., student, 2014-2016

Beyond just math, Mr. Fiore taught life. Alongside polynomials he brought another level to the equation. One that wasn't realized until years later in a college level history class, then again in a Calculus 2 class, and every so often in day to day life. What are the expectations for a math teacher in a middle school classroom? Well, as a teenager I probably could not care less. All I wanted was to finish up with school and avoid mathematics, if possible. However, when it came to Mr. Fiore's math class, he created a common language for discussing math in the classroom that allowed the student and the teacher to be on the same page. He was the only math instructor I have ever had that composed a curriculum that made understanding mathematics interesting and possible. Mr. Fiore can present a challenging and difficult mathematical concept clearly and logically. He uses plenty of examples when teaching, he has the expertise to relate his lectures to one another and demonstrate the relevance of two or more mathematical concepts, and he does this while ALWAYS remembering to put the student first and monitor their progress. One last thing that I can say about Mr. Fiore is that he has a way of motivating a student to come to class and work at the best of their abilities. He does this by establishing a sincere interest for the student. Mr. Fiore taught my mother, my sister, me, and my younger brother. He not only possesses a passion for mathematics and the material being taught, but he genuinely cares about the student's whole well-being. Mr. Fiore's mathematical abilities are attested by his earned respect from his students. Mr. Fiore is the BEST math teacher hands down! – Maria L., student, 2004-2005

Here are thoughts.... I always felt that if the kids I taught felt safe and happy when they came to school, then they were open to learning and exploring. I feel that if they felt safe, they would be ready to take risks. Risk taking is how they learn new things. Here is an example: If they are willing to take a risk and feel safe about doing it. They will sit down and write without worrying about how to spell a word or getting something wrong. Even very young children will just have at it. They have great ideas to share and being brave enough to just sit down and write down their thinking is so important. So, my first idea to share is that. Children feeling safe, secure, and happy to be in school help them learn to take risks which will help them learn. – Marilou N., teacher

His lessons on presentation and organization still reverberate with me thirteen years later. I was the kid with a backpack full of loose papers until I had him. As a math teacher he is exemplary. As a teacher that can see exactly what a student needs, he is astounding. I would like to take this opportunity to personally thank you for being such a great teacher so many years ago. Also, for being one of the first teachers to put me on the path to an intellectual awakening. – Mario C., student, 2002-2003

When it came to you and a few other teachers all of you had shown that you had care about us students by treating us like family and doing what was necessary when we were acting out negatively towards others. You guys expressed the acceptance of diversity in others and tried to make the best of your classes and you guys showed that you loved your job. – Matthew A., student, 2011-2012

Mr. Fiore is a teacher who is able to take complex ideas and explain them and extrapolate them in such a way that they are easily understood comprehended by any person, his passion for learning is what I admired about Mr. Fiore and his willingness to work with you till you grasp what he is trying to teach and his ability to be flexible in tutoring is exemplary. – Matthew H., student, 2004-2005

Never will forget the best mathematics teacher I've ever had the pleasure of being educated by. Thank you, Mr. Fiore...Just giving credit where credit is due sir. You are the best dang teacher I've ever had! – Matthew M., student, 2005-2006

You were a great teacher, by far the best teacher I ever had and my favorite. Not you only did you teach us math lessons, but you taught us life lessons, too. If a student needed help with something you always were there to count on. I'm very

grateful to say I had you as a teacher. Thank you, a lot! – Matthew M., student, 2014-2015

Mr. Fiore can teach a brick to float, given enough time. Fortunately for us, he was a math instructor and not a swim coach. As a result, he taught those same bricks math instead. His teaching ability was unmatched, and it was clear by his success rate (our class had an almost perfect honors rate). Mr. Fiore could have likely taught whatever subject he pleased if he was given time and information. His ability to relay the material in an easy-to-understand manner was a major factor in his students' success. This is critical to math instruction, and Mr. Fiore has it down to a science. I still find myself (at the time of writing this, in college calculus) using techniques and methods taught by Mr. Fiore. Now, with the changing curriculum for subjects, Mr. Fiore has proven in the classroom he is able to teach no matter the content and do so efficiently. The Common Core has proven to be a new challenge for students and teachers alike, but Mr. Fiore has met this challenge head-on and truly managed to help prepare students for this new curriculum. – Matthew T., student, 2010-2012

Hi, Mr. Fiore, so glad to hear from you. My input would be pertaining to all my teachers in the Lackawanna school system. I loved my school years. I remember wanting to go to school to learn because a lot of the teachers made it very interesting and fun, so I loved being in school. You are one of my favorites, whom I remember the most, because you made it fun and you kept our interest. You made algebra lovable!!! – Maureen M., student, 1979-1980

I believe that the most important characteristic of a teacher is to be understanding. To have an understanding that not all their students can simply drop their outside troubles once they enter the classroom and have complete focus. Life is harder for some than it is for others, and a minor problem for one person can be a huge setback for another. A great teacher makes room to work with their students and is sympathetic to their circumstances. While in college, I was diagnosed with social anxiety and major depression. While seeking help, I began to fall behind in my classes. I was stressed and ready to give up. I explained my situation to my professors and to my surprise they worked with me to make sure I could get my grades back up. I was given extensions on upcoming deadlines, permission to email them questions and concerns after office hours, and the encouragement I needed to jump back into my studies. The classroom can often be a challenging environment but having an understanding and flexible mentor can go a long way. – Maurisha H., student, 2006-2008

Mr. Fiore was the best kind of teacher you could have. He came in early, stayed late, and sacrificed those very valuable lunch breaks to help his students achieve. He had a way of making every student he worked with just as passionate about succeeding as he was about teaching. To this day, throughout high school and college, and the start of my very own teaching career, I have never been in a classroom that was more driven and goal oriented than his math class. All that was due to his passion and leadership. He is one of the people who inspired me to become a teacher and showed me teaching is about believing in your students and supporting in every way you can. Anyone who can be taught by Peter Fiore will be better off because of it. – Megan S., student, 2003-2006

Well, as you know, you are and always will be my favorite teacher. The thing I remember most and will always remember about you, is that we were your first advanced class... It was trial and error for all of us... You recognized that what we were doing wasn't working and we regrouped and found methods that worked. In other words, you weren't stuck in your ways. You adjusted to us, and we ended up thriving from the adjustments. I always will remember and admire that. Also, you didn't talk down to us... You made your position of authority known, but you were always respectful. – Melissa W., student, 2001-2002

I honestly loved every minute of your class. I went from flunking the first quiz you gave to getting 90s throughout the two years I had you. You are honestly the best teacher I have ever had. You cared about all of us and truly tried helping every student that has walked through your doors. It was truly an honor to be your student for two years. – Michael C., student, 2009-2011

Mr. Fiore is by far one of the best math teachers out there. His personality is like no other. He's fun, energetic (even at 7AM), and he genuinely cares about his students. If you need extra help, he provides it with no hesitation. If you are struggling, he motivates you to do better. No students are left behind when it comes to Mr. Fiore. – Michael H., student, 2009-2011

With the implantation of Common Core across the nation, many students, parents, and teachers alike are becoming increasingly frustrated and overwhelmed with the erroneous standards and guidelines being forced upon them. However, if there is one individual that can alleviate this academic irritation, it is Mr. Peter Fiore. As a former instructor of mine, Mr. Fiore has provided me with countless hours of enlightenment that remains unparalleled; allocating time after school hours to ensure that I understood the material unequivocally as well as transforming the coursework into palatable assignments that were far easier to comprehend as opposed to their textbook counterparts. He has continuously and tirelessly dedicated himself to the field of Mathematics when others shuddered at the thought of teaching such a subject, all while making it look like a walk in the park. Mr. Fiore is far more than an educational instructor; he is a mentor that offers success to anyone who is willing to work for it. He has given me more in life than I than I can ever hope to repay, and for that I am eternally grateful. – Michael W., student, 2006-2008

As a previous student to Lackawanna Middle School, with a below par math skill set at the time, it was extremely difficult for me to grasp math to figure out a solution to a problem. Now, as a machinist who uses math daily, I would like to say thank you, Mr. Fiore, and best wishes on your new journey. – Michael Z., student, 2002-2003

There is no doubt that you love what you do. Your passion and methods of teaching have brought out the best in all of us. If you need help with Math, Mr. Fiore is your solution. Best teacher I ever had, hands down! – Nicholas W., student, 2006-2008

Hey, Mr. Fiore. First off, I want to say I hope everything is great & hope nothing but the best for my favorite math teacher of all time. Second, I would like to say congratulations on this book. It'll be a good one. But the most important characteristics of a teacher with me is building a relationship with his/her students. I feel like when a teacher builds a bond with a class & is very thorough about what exactly him/her is teaching. & that's why I loved your class so much! Yes, you made class very fun & easy as possible for your students, but you weren't afraid to get in our ass if we were slacking off or not working to our potential. You were like a motivator & a friend. A lot of teachers just want to get what they have to say out there & not really care if the class LEARNED anything. I feel like you must have a passion for what you do in life whether it's teaching or plumbing or engineering etc. as a student, I love a teacher who makes the environment comfortable for their students. but also make sure they LEARN. That's why I love you, Mr. Fiore! – Nicholas W., student, 2013-2014

Mr. Fiore, math has never been my strong point. It never came as easy to me as other subjects. But it was different when you were my teacher. The way you taught was much easier for me to understand and I enjoyed those two years I had you as a teacher. Honestly, you were one of the few math teachers I could learn math from. Anything after those two years were somewhat of a struggle for me. I've always felt comfortable coming to you for help and you were always happy to help. Thanks for all the knowledge you provided me and all the other students at LMS and LHS. – Nicolas R., student, 2007-2009

I always thought you were an amazing teacher. I truly never liked Math because I never understood it, until I started my 8th grade year at LMS. You would know when I wouldn't understand what you were teaching by my facial expressions. You would go out of your way to make sure I understood the problem. I will forever remember my 8th grade math teacher. – Nicole C., student, 2008-2009

I had a pleasure to be in Mr. Fiore's Math class in 8th and it was the best class I had throughout the day (besides band and chorus). I would always come back to his class even if I already had my class with him. He always participated in the school's activities and always cared about the students and their family. Especially the music department. Mr. Fiore, Mr. Rice and Mrs. Schuh encouraged me to do the pit band in the musical and it was AMAZING. Because of Mr. Fiore I have my life on track. Most Outstanding Math Teacher. – Nicole V., student, 2013-2014

8th grade year and I'm going into the 4th quarter with a 79 overall average and the best teacher ever not only helps me but helps me have the biggest comeback getting my grade point average from an abysmal 79 all the way up to a 92 and scoring a 92 on the final exam as well, that's just one story. But you're just a great teacher, you get along with the students well and tell us stories to keep us entertained. You don't have favorites nor pick on anyway and you're well respected by everyone you've ever taught, even the kids that didn't care can't deny of not only good of a teacher you are but how wise and sincere you can be as well. You taught me a lot of things besides math including things in sports, life, great advice giver for sure, I think you get that from your wife lol, but just one of the greatest humans beings I'll ever encounter in my lifetime and I'm honored that I had the pleasure to be taught, tutored, and mentored by you on many separate occasions. I wish your book success and I know it'll be great. I love you Mr. Fiore, and I appreciate EVERYTHING you've done for my brother and me. – Noble S., student, 2013-2014

The most important characteristic of a teacher to me was one I didn't recognize at the time. It was certainly innate as I look back and still is as I look towards my six children and their various experiences. Who I consider my best and most efficacious teachers, who I hear the most thoughtful commentary from my children even years later were individuals with some common thread? The most important characteristic was love. They truly love what they are doing through the ups, downs twist and turns. They truly care for the student's welfare, caring not only about teaching the subjects, but being a good example and somehow overlapping good life lessons without the student even knowing at the time. They were always looking for the opportunity to teach. This love helped them to be kind, tough when they needed and only when they needed to be, NOT to brag, be unbecoming or jealous of another because their focus was 100% outward. When I look back at my own experience, I see they didn't hold grudges regarding the wrongs they suffered but still managed daily to endure with hope and a never fading belief in their mission. Even though a teacher knows they won't see the real fruit of their labors for years the best ones find satisfaction in smaller present successes because they aren't only always looking for the opportunity to teach but to encourage the students and help them believe in themselves. Those little sparks, and occasionally a bigger one, keep the good teacher not only anchored in the day but reminded of the larger picture. They keep them smiling. Ultimately, it's not about the subject but the subject. By that I mean it's not about the math, science or whatever subject it's about the people. To the best teachers, students are people and the subjects they are concerned most about. I'm 54, have an undergraduate BS, have one child with a master's degree, one in a master's program, one a sophomore in college, one whom college was not right for, one with special needs who graduated high school and one who is a junior in high school. To all of us the best teachers never change. We run across them in our lives and they seem like a time machine. If asked I'm sure they would say teaching is not what I do, it's who I am. – Paul M., parent

He is not only an educator of mathematics in the classroom, for he is also a remarkable life coach. In a world where crime and violence are constantly on the rise, it is Mr. Fiore that preached teamwork and love for your fellow students. I believe that he made one of largest impacts on violence in my school; where misbehavior is more than common.

The words "give up" do not exist in Mr. Fiore's immeasurable personal dictionary. This was one of his many lessons he preached during his daily class sermons on how to handle life's hardships. It is without a doubt that he "set the tone" for my

career as a student and facilitated my positive attitude when approaching difficult obstacles in life. Having since finished high school as salutatorian, graduated from the University at Buffalo with a BS in Biology, currently in a Master's program, and applying to UB's medical school next June, it is here where I credit this extraordinary man for laying the foundation for which I built my personal success, not only an academic student, but as a young adult. – Petar P., student, 2005-2007

To say Mr. Fiore is a great teacher would be too much of an understatement. I've been to three different colleges and high school, and I've never had a teacher make an impression on me as great as his. I've never met a teacher that takes time out to stop being a teacher and get to know his students, their weaknesses and their strong points. I loved coming to his class every single day. Mr. Fiore is a great teacher, mentor and friend for life! If you are lucky enough to have his class, I'm pretty sure you will not only become a better student, but you will become a better person! – Quinten W., student, 2002-2003

As a student I loved being able to show up in a classroom where it felt like a home away from home. Community, connection, diversity, humility, perseverance, character development, fun and LAUGHTER were some of the many things that class with Mr. Fiore offered. So many years later, now a parent myself, I look for the qualities of him and many other amazing teachers throughout my educational journey, in my children's teachers. Of all the jobs in the world, being a teacher is amongst the hardest ones. "Education is what survives when what has been learned has been forgotten". (B.F. Skinner) – Quintia R., student, 2002-2003

As a novice educator, I often find myself asking what qualities I would hope to possess that past teachers have had which I've admired the most. For you, Mr. Fiore - this is easy. Your passion, diligence, and innovativeness to motivate students is unmatched and has stuck with me for the past 13 years. Math (especially the NEW Math) can be difficult for several reasons. However, you were always able to explain material in an engaging way and make sense of what was thought to be impossible at first glance.

We are students from the day we are born and all throughout our lives. Being a student evokes curiosity, employs critical thinking, and challenges what we already know. To be a student and to learn is one of the simplest joys in life – a joy that can only be amplified when we learn from a teacher who resembles a mentor more than anything. Teachers who not only cover content, but offer guidance and encouragement are those we learn the most from – about the material being presented and more importantly about our own capabilities. My experience has taught me that the most important characteristics of a teacher are passion and patience. When we sense that a teacher cares about us and our success, we can let go of insecurities and push ourselves to achieve the very things our teacher already knows we can attain. This is what it takes to be a remarkable teacher and to have an impact on a student throughout his/her entire life. – Rada S., student, 2004-2005

No matter the situation at hand, you consistently put your students first. You did anything and everything necessary to assure that they were on the right path. In fact, you were the first and only teacher to ever make me want to do homework. Your passion and intellect are unmatched. – Raymond M., student, 2010-2012

As a student the most important characteristics of a teacher is patience and understanding. Having the patience to work with a student who may not understand something as quickly as their students in class. Understanding that some kids learn more effectively in other ways. – Renee A., student, 2004-2005

Where to start? Mr. Fiore has always gone above and beyond to help a student pass an exam, or to help the drama club or sports teams at Lackawanna High School. Mr. Fiore never had me as a student; but that didn't stop him from helping me to understand math or to have a conversation about college and what I am majoring in at SUNY Fredonia. This man (Peter Fiore) has donated so much of his own time to do the announcing for any home football and basketball games. If it was not for Mr. Fiore's encouragement, I do not think I could have passed the geometry exam after all the attempts I had previously taken. Mr. Fiore does more for the Lackawanna School System than most present-day teachers have! There is no person with as much passion for the community or the school system, or the need to help a civilian (school student or neighbor) with any question or problem. Mr. Fiore will always be the best math teacher at Lackawanna Middle/High Schools. Thank you, Mr. Fiore, for all your guidance and knowledge of Math to help me succeed in school. One thing that stands out is that this man does not put up with tom foolery from anybody. Mr. Fiore acts, not a trip to the principal's office. If anyone wonders what word there is to describe him, the answers most likely are caring, inspirational, helpful, determined, and, most of all, a friend. Thank you for your services teaching groups of successful and talented children, Mr. Fiore. I am sure that their careers are going to be amazing after all your time and efforts. Thank you for being a kind and humble man, Mr. Peter Fiore! – Robert P., student

I feel like a big part of being a good teacher is being able to not take things personally. A lot of the time, at least in my experience, a teacher will hold a grudge against a student because they feel disrespected by the kid talking in class or sleeping through a lesson. Then they end up having a short fuse for that student and end up treating them more harshly. It contributes absolutely nothing to their education and just makes it harder on everyone. The teacher gets stressed and then the kid doesn't even want to be there and is less likely to pay attention as a result. Really the same problems with society in general plague the educational system. People forget to be understanding and it makes it miserable for everyone. Another thing that makes a good teacher out of a bad one and brings a good teacher to star status is giving real world examples for the subject matter. I'm sure you're all too familiar with the phrase, "when am I even going to need to know this?" A good way to do that IMO would be relating the subject to a profession and explaining how the concept is used in said profession. That would also help end the problem many students face at the end of their school career of not having any clue what they want to do with their lives. If every teacher did that for every subject, then kids would know not only what they're good at but also how to apply that to something they enjoy. Better than any special technique or quick tip though, just treat the students like people. Don't look at them as people subject to your authority, that's the biggest problem I've had with teachers. It goes from bad to worse in a hurry when you use a position of authority to make it known you have authority. – Robert S., student, 2007-2009

I taught with Peter Fiore in the same building for over 15 years, but never had the pleasure of teaching in his classroom with him until this past year. I am a special education teacher and this past year I was assigned with my students to Peter's pre- algebra class. I always heard from others and watched from a distance how Peter welcomed and assisted all students, whether assigned to his class or not, but this year I had the chance to experience this myself. Each day Mr. Fiore started class on a personal level. He talked about his family, sports, and asked his students what they would like to share. When the lesson started for the day, he engaged students, not just giving the answer but showing them how he got the answer and giving them alternate ways to solve problems. Mr. Fiore made sure the students knew the material before moving on. He walked around and assured the students that they could do this and then offered his free periods to work one on one. I then knew why everyone wanted Mr. Fiore as their teacher. He was not just a good math teacher, but a person who cared enough to share his personal life and was genuinely concerned that they learned math no matter what it took. Unfortunately for our school district Mr. Fiore retired, but when he left, he made sure that the students of Lackawanna knew he was always just a phone call away. I would recommend Peter Fiore to anyone who needs a math tutor. I am so glad that I had the chance to work with him and see for myself daily just what he means to his students and why. – Roberta L., teacher

Hey there, Mr. Fiore. It's taken me a few days to think the characteristics of a good teacher through as they pertain to you. You respected every student and treated us like we were adults. You were extremely kind and right by my side when I needed your help you were there as a teacher but when you taught it was unlike anything I'd experienced prior, You wanted to be there, you didn't blow through the material, you took your time and made sure everyone understood what they *needed. One of your best and most important characteristics was patience. You didn't let everyone get under your skin. You made the learning environment fun me and my friends at the time looked forward to your class. You made such a great impact on our school, and we talk about you even today. I strongly believe I will never meet another teacher like you in this lifetime, but it was in honor to have a seat in your class. So, a quick rundown of characteristics. Patience, Kindness, Respect, Strong Will And the want to be there Those are important characteristics of a good teacher. If I had to name a few more that describe you I'd say passion you loved your job while it seemed that every other teacher hated theirs. To me at least you seemed like the father figure I wanted in my life. I strived to impress you. You gave me the want to do well. Today I've got nothing below a 95 and I thank you for that. I thank you for steering me down the right path. I am forever grateful.* – Ryan L., student, 2014-2016*

Mr. Fiore helped me with Common Core math when I moved here in April. I came from a state that never had Common Core. In those two to three months he helped me understand how Common Core works and he helped me pass my exam with flying colors. Mr. Fiore showed me how to do the problem and helped me understand the concepts of the question and how to solve them. – Samantha K., student, 2015-2016

As a special education teacher at Lackawanna Middle School I have worked with Mr. Peter Fiore for several years. He has not only a great knowledge of the subject of math, but also creative and effective ways in which to teach the many topics in the math curriculum. His strategies and demonstrations help all students including those having difficulties grasping the concepts. – Sandra L., teacher

Mr. Fiore was an amazing math teacher. He was so helpful. Math was always my worst subject, as I never understood it until Mr. Fiore was my teacher. He explains the material in ways other teachers can't seem to do. He's always willing to help you when you need it. I never even liked to go to math class except for when I had Mr. Fiore. I always looked forward to his class. He made math seem so simple.

Thank you for all you do and being an amazing teacher. – Santina G., student, 2014-2015

Every time I'm in a store and my friend asks what's 20% of the overall price, I reflect to the middle school years when you taught us how to figure out which coupon would be better to use. A small memory but a life lesson. You are always supportive of your students and impacted every one of us in a positive way. The most important characteristic for a teacher, in my opinion, would be dedication. Teaching is more than just an 8-4 job; it involves year-round dedication. Students thrive off good support system at school, in which teachers want to see us succeed and establish solid relationships. For some students, a teacher is their outlet and a mentor (especially in my case). Most of the teachers at Lackawanna wanted to make sure I worked to the best of my potential even after I graduated. Looking into colleges was tough for me when my parents didn't have that background. Many teachers at LHS go the extra mile to make sure we pass our regents exams, graduate on time, etc. Patience is also an important characteristic to have. Ultimately, those two go hand in hand, but you know teachers really care (especially in your case) when they show up to outside activities to support us in that way as well whether sports, musicals, or concerts.

I'm not sure if you are still writing the book, but if you are the characteristics that I like in teachers are the ones who can keep the whole classes attention and still teach. That the students can learn everyday even if it means not teaching 40 minutes straight. Ways to explain the topic so that everyone understands even if that means a few days on the topic. That is just what I noticed. I hope this helps. – Sarah B., 2010-2012

You were the only Math teacher I had that helped me to understand Math. – Sarah H., student, 2007-2008

A wonderful caring and honorable teacher that has been there for me in and out of the class and has touched my life when it came down to my home life while I took care of my mom and my own health issues. To take a day out of your time to transfer me to and from the ER with my mother's consent. A great guy with a big heart. The best teacher I've ever had an encounter with. On every note I still hold positive memories in the classroom and outside of it as well. – Shania M., student, 2015-2016

Teachers must show they care about every one of their students. I mean school was not easy for me at all. The teachers who showed they cared and helped me are the classes I passed. If the teacher shows little to no effort it is hard for a student to really pay attention. My kids are just like me. If they cannot see the fun in something, they have no interest in learning it. Just like if a child has a learning disability it makes it easy for that child to want to want to give up. Like me. I read backwards whether it is a book and even my numbers if a teacher does not take the time to help that person what is the sense? I dropped out of school for that reason. Therefore, a teacher that shows they really care are the ones who need to stick around. I hope that helped as little bit. I haven't had coffee, so my thought process is not all there yet. – Sibbie W., student, 2007-2008

Mr. Fiore was my math teacher for 8th grade. I wish he was my math teacher for 9th grade. Before I was in Mr. Fiore's class, I was failing math, badly, but he helped me understand math. He is so helpful. If you had a problem Mr. Fiore was the man to go to. You need help he was there for you. You wanted someone to talk to, Mr. Fiore was there. I honestly could not thank him enough for everything he's helped me with. Thank you, Mr. Fiore, for helping me and my fellow classmates with our extremely confusing Common Core math. – Skylar R., student, 2014-2015

I had the pleasure of taking Mr. Fiore's advanced math class in 7th grade and was intrigued by the challenge. My older brother who had him the year prior said nothing but kind words about him. It is one thing to hear about his greatness as a teacher but another thing to experience it first-hand. Mr. Fiore's passion to his craft and the success of his students shined bright every single day that I stepped into his classroom. His attention to detail and ability to modify his teaching style to each specific student to ensure their academic success was what made him the "cool" math teacher that I heard so much about. Being a teacher is not an easy job by any means, and to continually wake up every day and devote your life to creating a positive change in his students' lives is what Mr. Fiore did so naturally. It was an honor to learn from him and be a student on his Wall of Fame. – Smajil M., student, 2004-2005

Passionate. Passionate about teaching and about your students. Didn't just teach us to pass a test, you cared that we learned. A great mentor and role model and glad to have been in your class. – Stephanie F., student, 2001-2002

Mr. Fiore is by far the best teacher I have ever had. He explains stuff in a way where it is a lot more understanding. He will go far beyond what he must in order to make sure each of his students understands the material. He stays after school more than any teacher I know to make sure his students know the material. I would understand something he taught instantly, but when a different teacher explained it, I got confused and this is a totally real story. My best Math grades occurred while I was in Mr. Fiore's class. Mr. Fiore is the best teacher and most helpful teacher I've ever had. – Steven R., student, 2014-2015

Mr. Fiore was by far one of my favorite teachers all throughout my educational career. He expected a lot out of his students but in a way where we never felt too pressured. You could tell he always genuinely cared about his students and seemed to be able to get the best out of us. He was always a fair person and a fair teacher. There are not too many people that I respect more than Mr. Fiore, not only as a teacher, but as a person as well. – Steven S., student, 2007-2009

Well to me the most important thing to me with teaching was having a teacher that was involved, I mean a teacher that just hands out a worksheet for a day and sits behind a desk. A teacher that is up in front of class involved and working out *the lesson with the class is a more impactful one in my opinion. I will never forget you as a teacher and I will always remember you as one of the greatest teachers I've ever known. Not just for your ability to stay on lesson and be involved with your students but also your ability to be involved with their personal life as well. You knew each one of your students whether they were in one of your classes on a professional personal level which made you be able to adapt to each student to know what would make them learn the best. As I'm much older than 7th and 8th grade math class with you I can see how much work an amazing teacher like you and a few others puts in to make the learning environment an impactful one for students. You were so involved with the school district and you still are its amazing. I still see you post about the sporting events. I am thinking about maybe pursuing a teaching career later in life and I will look back at your teachings as a way I would run my class.* – Steven W., student, 2009-2011

"Nothing is unattainable." A well-fitting motto that comes to mind when describing my educational experience with Mr. Peter Fiore. Day in and day out, Mr. Fiore came to work and performed his duties as an educator with extreme professionalism and passion. May it be complex math equations or the endless life guidance that all young adults seek, Mr. Fiore ensured EVERY student in his classroom strived to obtain the best possible solutions. Never was an "I don't know" acceptable in the classrooms of Mr. Peter Fiore. With excellent educational strategies Mr. Fiore successfully implemented mathematical content and developed the critical confidence that I needed as a student to learn mathematics. His endless drive in guiding the future generations that sat in the seats before him towards success has set the bar through the roof for all educators. Advanced Algebra or adolescent advice, class was always in session. Peter Fiore has cemented his legacy in the Educational Hall of Fame. – Sulaiman M., student, 2004-2005

Peter Fiore is by far the best teacher and mentor I have ever had. He was able to make some of the most difficult topics simple and explain them in a way that was easy to understand. His teaching style, attitude, and dedication have stuck with me. It is over a decade later and I can honestly say that, after high school and 6 years of college, no other teacher I've had has shown the amount of dedication, interest, and understanding in their students like Mr. Fiore. – Susan E., student, 2003-2006

Out of all the teachers that I've had, I would have to say that Mr. Fiore is one of the best. He is the reason why math became my favorite subject. Any person can agree that when Mr. Fiore would teach a class you can feel how compassionate he was in teaching his students. He made it easy, fun, interesting and always kept a positive attitude. He gives you the support and push a student should have from a teacher. Mr. Fiore has the essentials I feel every teacher should have when teaching students. He puts in the time and effort in order to make sure that you get down all the necessary skills needed to pass a test. Thanks for being an awesome teacher and role model. - Symone R., student, 2003-2004

Mr. Fiore is HANDS DOWN the best teacher I've ever had. I'm deplorable at Math. I never liked the subject at all and got bad grades. Then, in 8th grade, that completely changed. He was able to explain Math to me in a way I could understand and because of his tremendous teaching ability, I maintained consistently good grades all year. He is the only teacher I've ever had that had the patience and willingness to sit and work with you to make sure you understood the lesson. One of the best things about him is his dedication to the students' education. He really cares and shows it in a way I've never seen another teacher do. In my opinion, Mr. Peter Fiore is the best teacher to have ever taught in the Lackawanna school system. – Tevin S., student, 2006-2007

A good teacher is someone who can make a subject you hate so much your favorite class of the day not just because of pizza & friends but it's your favorite because you enjoy the teacher & the material. A good teacher is someone who knows how to teach well enough that you improve on every weekly test you take & you take those tests home to your mom & she's proud of you cause you're doing so well & actually genuinely enjoy going to school every day. – Timothy J., student, 2013-2014

The way you taught the class was perfect and I really learned a lot in your class with how you were as a teacher. I remember you telling stories at the start of classes and some of them stayed with me and you would do work on the overhead and I remember coming to you before summer telling you I was horrible at math and you turned me around the next school year. I wish I had you as a math teacher every year. – Trent S., student, 2014-2015

Math has always been one of my favorite subjects but as I got into harder math every year, I started to hate it. But I have to say the most superb math teacher I have ever had was Peter Fiore. He delivered mathematical techniques in a way that was easy to follow and understand and made it so much fun to learn. I never forgot anything he ever taught me, and I am so thankful I had the opportunity to work with him.

I have a few qualities I look for in a good teacher. I respect a teacher that has empathy and reaches out to the student and is observant to absences and possible out of class issues and tries to take that into consideration and help in anyway. I enjoy classes that are fun in a sense that the teacher is professional but can joke around and make the students comfortable in that learning environment. I also really like when the teacher caters to all the different learning types. Using different tools to get the curriculum across for the visual, auditory and kinesthetic learners as well the ones with learning disabilities. Finally, I really enjoy a class no matter what the topic if the teacher clearly shows their passion for what they're teaching. If they show that they don't care about it, the students don't care either. Being completely honest, you were one of the best teachers I've ever had! You had/have every trait of a great teacher and I remember not pulling my weight as a student and you pulled me aside and told me you noticed something wasn't right. I learned things so easily, so quickly, and thoroughly in your class. To this day algebra is still my favorite because of my experience. – Uniqua R., student, 2010-2012

I remember when you used to be my teacher you always gave us advice about life and how to be a better person in and out of school. Honestly, I really appreciate that, and I think that was one of your best characteristics. – Waleed A., student, 2003-2004

I learn best when I enjoy the subject I'm learning. For example, I've always been interested in the sciences and so I would pay more attention in class. It was something I wanted to learn about, so maybe you need to convince the students that they will enjoy what you teach them (or at least increase their interest in the subject from negative and indifferent to at least slightly positive). -I learn best with examples. Sometimes (in math) I won't understand how to do a problem after it's explained. But if the teacher goes through several slightly different examples, I can get a better understanding of the process used to solve a problem.
— Xavier K., student, 2012-2013

I may be a bit late, but I did see that you are writing a book about your teaching history. I just wanted to let you know how much you inspired me having me in your 8th grade Advanced class. I had an amazing experience with you. I remember I was in 7th grade regular math, and my only dream at the time was to be in Mr. Fiore's Advanced math class. My sister was in your class and I recall being so jealous whenever she would come home and tell us stories about your class, and how well you taught and how funny you were. I came to you a few times throughout the year to get encouragement and motivation to get into your class. You told me to work hard and be at the top of my current class, and that's what I did. I got the highest scores and worked my butt off, and anytime I had a problem I came to you and you weren't even my teacher yet. You helped me solve my difficult problems. I remember distinctly that I had a 99% average and Mr. Fischer told me that, if I solved a problem, he would give me extra credit to raise my average to 100%. Unfortunately, I was stuck so I came to you. You didn't give me the answer, but instead you led me to it. You showed me that if I pushed myself, I could find it on my own, and I did. I got the 100% average for that quarter and was named the school's Student of the Quarter in Math. I had always looked up to you, but when you helped me with that question, I knew you had to be my next teacher. You taught us to use our brains and trust our instincts.

At the end of the year I was ecstatic when Mr. Fischer told me that he had recommended me for 8th grade Advanced Math. When I got to your class, it was a bit intense to see whose name would make it on the Honor Board after a test, but you knew I could do it. Hell, you knew we could all do it. To this day I always bring you up when talking to my husband about my school experience, and how you were my favorite teacher. I just wanted to give you my input and my personal experience and how you inspired me. I just though you should know. Thank you, Mr. Fiore, thank you so much. – Xena M., student, 2010-2011